WELCOMING GUESTS

Center Piece

Instructions on page 41

Tablecloth
Instructions on page 42

Center Piece
Instructions on page 43

Luncheon Mats & Napkins

Instructions on page 45

Framed Picture
Instructions on page 46

Piano Throw
Instructions on page 48

Framed Picture
Instructions on page 56

Pillows
Instructions on page 50

Panels
Instructions on page 51

Pillow
Instructions on page 53

IDEAS FOR COMFORT

Runner
Instructions on page 55

Album
Instructions on page 58

17

Center Piece
Instructions on page 60

Small Pictures
Instructions on page 62

GOOD MORNING

Caps of Jam Jar Labels Coasters

Tray Mat

Instructions on page 65 for Caps of Jam Jar & Labels, on page 63 for Coasters, on page 66 for Tray Mat

PERSONALLY YOURS

Bedspread
Instructions on page 70

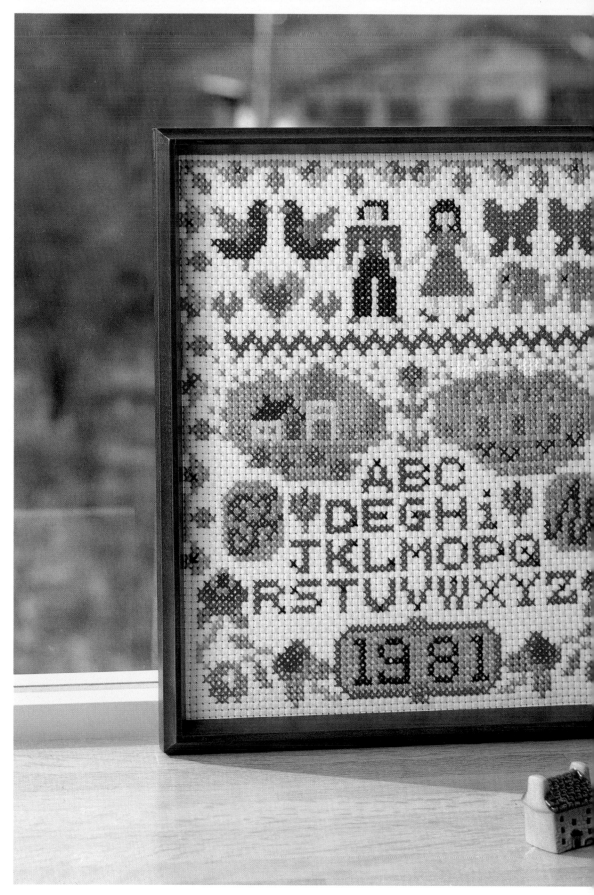

Framed Pictures
Instructions on page 68

March, march.
Head erect.
Left, right,
That's correct.

LOOKING BACK
TO CHILDHOOD

Pincushions
Instructions on page 74

Pochettes Spectacle Case Vanity Case Pen Case Box Jacket

Instructions on page 77 for Spectacle Case & Vanity Case
& Pen Case & Box Jacket, on page 80 for Pochettes

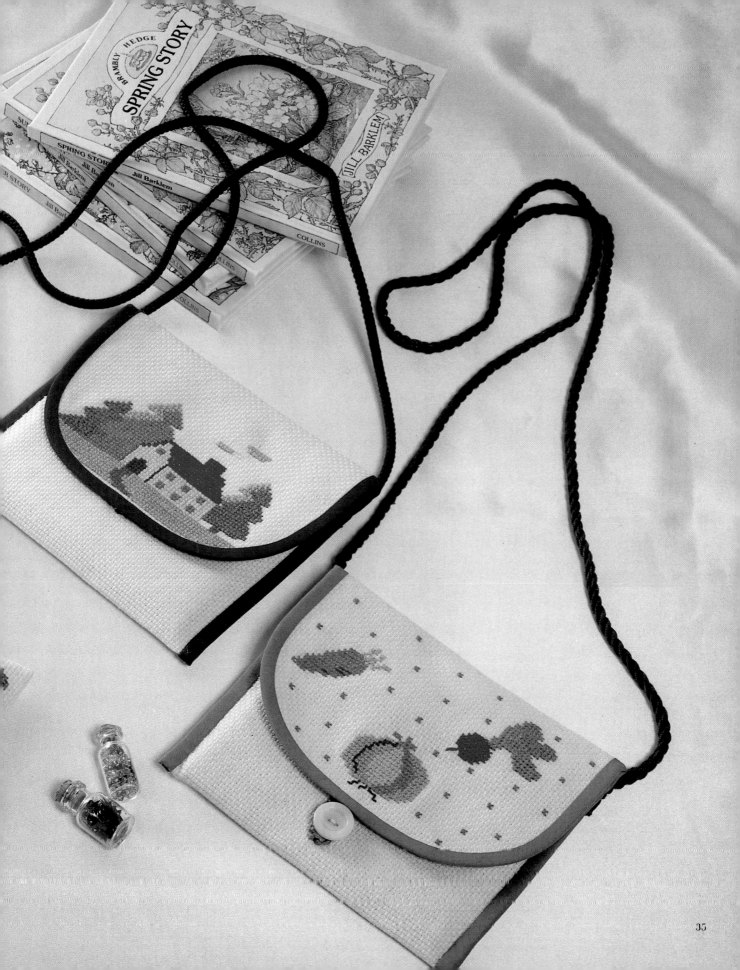

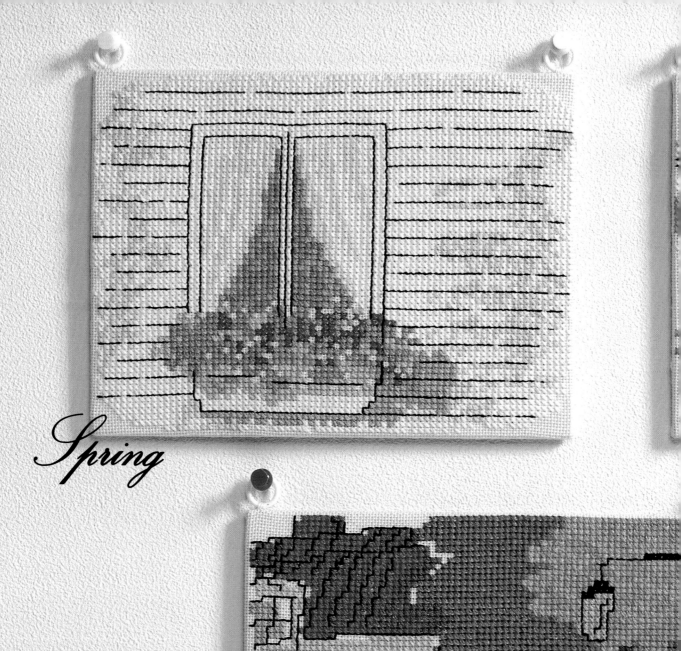

Spring

Panels
Instructions on page 81

Summer

Autumn

Winter

Small Sack Vanity Case Pouch
Bags for Lessons

Instructions on page 85 for Small Sack, on page 86 for
Vanity Case, on page 87 for Pouch, on page 88 for Bags
for Lessons

Divider with Pockets
Instructions on page 90

MAKING INSTRUCTIONS

CENTER PIECE　　　shown on page 1

Center

With 3 strands

☒	=	640
⬤	=	936
◉	=	758
Ⓣ	=	950
Ⓤ	=	320
◑	=	320
△	=	738
◇	=	3689
▦	=	471
◢	=	3685
◪	=	710

You'll Need:
- Fabric . . . Indian Cloth (10 cm of fabric = 52 square meshes) 59 cm square Beige.
- Threads . . . D.M.C 6-strand embroidery floss:
  9 skeins of Moss Green (469); 6 skeins of Moss Green (471); 3½ skeins of Smoke Grey (640); 2 skeins each of Moss Green (936), Pistachio Green (320); 1 skein of Raspberry Red (3685); ½ skein each of Terra-cotta (758), Chestnut (950), Umber (738) and Episcopal Purple (718); small amount of Raspberry Red (3689).
- Fittings . . . Crochet hook size 2/0

Finished Size: 61 cm in diameter
Size of Stitch: 1 square of design = 1 square mesh of fabric
Making Instructions:
  Cut fabric in shape, stitch embroidery, matching center of fabric to that of design. Turn allowance to wrong side, crochet edging along.

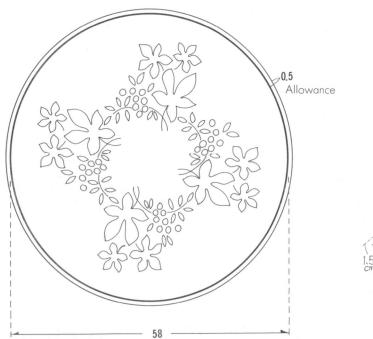

0.5 Allowance

58

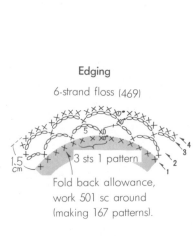

Edging

6-strand floss (469)

5

1.5 cm

3 sts 1 pattern

1
2
3
4

Fold back allowance, work 501 sc around (making 167 patterns).

TABLECLOTH shown on pages 2 – 3

You'll Need:
- Fabric . . . Java Cloth (10 cm of fabric = 35 square meshes) 90 cm square Beige.
- Threads . . . D.M.C 6-strand embroidery floss:
  3½ skeins of Hazel-nut Brown (422); 2½ skeins of Pistachio Green (320); 2 skeins of Parma Violet (208), Saffron (727); 1½ skeins each of Parma Violet (211), Saffron (725, 726), Garnet Red (335), Pistachio Green (368), Sage Green (3013); 1 skein each of Parma Violet (209), Garnet Red (309), Soft Pink (776, 819), Sage Green (3012); ½ skein each of Moss Green (469, 472), Indian Red (3042), Scarlet (304) and Umber (433, 739).

Finished Size: 80 cm square
Size of Stitch: 1 square of design = 1 square mesh of fabric
Making Instructions:
  Stitch embroidery, matching center of fabric to that of design. Fold back allowance twice mitering at corners (refer to page 95), finish with one-side hem-stitching.

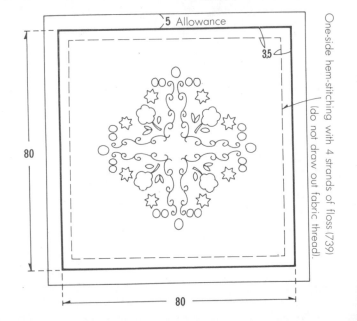

5 Allowance

3.5

80

80

One-side hem-stitching with 4 strands of floss (739)
(do not draw out fabric thread)

With 6 strands

− = 211		I = 819
⊠ = 209		● = 320
◆ = 208		▨ = 320
＋ = 3042		U = 368
⊥ = 727		△ = 469
○ = 726		V = 472
◖ = 725		L = 3013
■ = 304		Z = 3012
⊠ = 309		▲ = 433
Ａ = 335		⊙ = 422
⁄ = 776		

Center

CENTER PIECE   shown on pages 4 – 5

You'll Need:
- Fabric . . . Java cloth (10 cm of fabric = 35 square meshes) 87 cm by 45 cm Beige.
- Threads . . . D.M.C 6-strand embroidery floss: 2 skeins each of Copper Green (831), Umber (738); 1½ skeins each of Sevres Blue (799, 800), Forget-me-not Blue (809), Tangerine Yellow (742, 743), Copper Green (830), Soft Pink (776), Almond Green (502), Umber (436); 1 skein each of Magenta Rose (961), Tangerine Yellow (740), Moss Green (469, 471), Yellow Green (733), Almond Green (503), White; ½ skein each of Garnet Red (309), Magenta Rose (962, 963), Moss Green (935, 470), Sage Green (3013), Ivy Green (501), Sevres Blue (798); small amount each of Golden Yellow (783), Saffron (726) and Umber Gold (976).
- Fittings . . . 230 cm each of 4 cm wide Beige lace, 1.2 cm wide Beige bias tape.

Finished Size: 92 cm by 50 cm

Center →

Size of Stitch: 1 square of design = 1 square mesh of fabric

Making Instructions:
Stitch embroidery, matching center of fabric to that of design. Finish raw edge applying lace along.

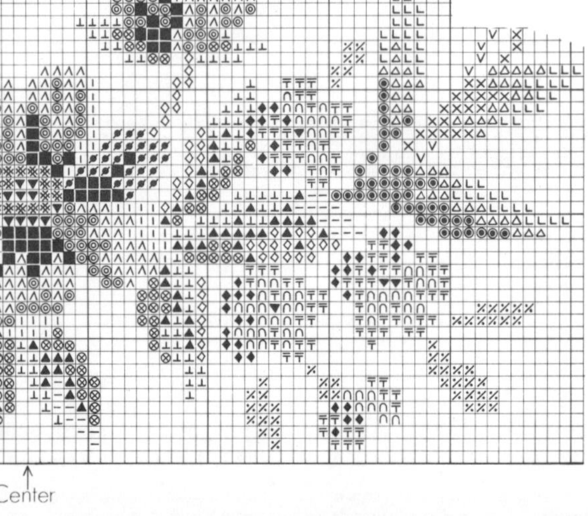

With 6 strands

Symbol	Color
■	= 309
◎	= 961
◪	= 962
∧	= 776
Ⅰ	= 963
⊠	= 798
●	= 799
+	= 809
⊿	= 800
O	= White
◆	= 740
⊤	= 742
∩	= 743
▼	= 976
⊖	= 783
⊞	= 726
▲	= 935
⊗	= 469
◇	= 470
⊥	= 471
⊟	= 3013
◉	= 830
✕	= 831
△	= 436
L	= 738
⑪	= 501
V	= 502
⅔	= 733
⊤	= 503

15
7.5
17
85
43
0.8 Allowance
Embroidery position

To Sew on Lace

Lace
3.5cm
0.8cm
① Put lace between, seam right sides together
② Slip st.
Bias tape (make the width narrow). (Wrong side)

↑ **Center**

44

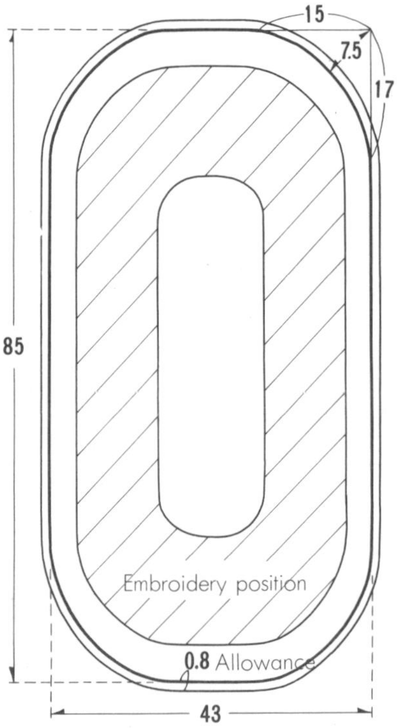

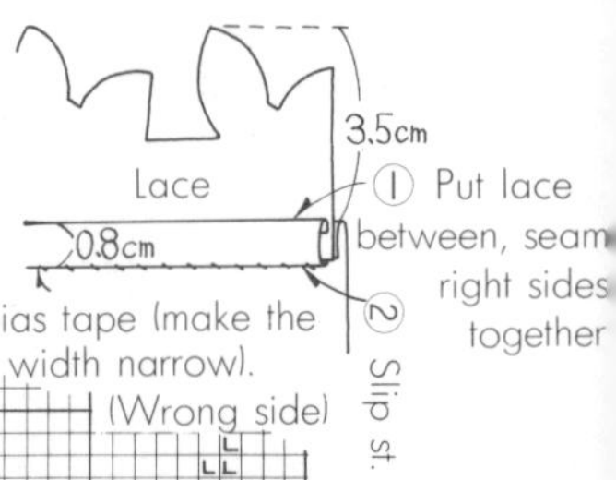

Luncheon mat:

You'll Need (for 2 pieces):
- Fabric . . . Java cloth (10 cm of fabric = 35 square meshes) 90 cm by 112 cm White.
- Threads . . . D.M.C 6-strand embroidery floss:
  9 skeins of Plum (554); 7 skeins of Brilliant Green (703);

4½ skeins of Royal Blue (995); 4 skeins each of Emerald Green (910), Beige (3032), Plum (552); 2 skeins each of Lemon Yellow (307) and Azure Blue (3325).

Finished Size: 104.5 cm by 38 cm

Size of Stitch: 1 square of design = 1 square mesh of fabric

With 5 strands unless specified.

○ = 307	△ = 3023
■ = 910	✕ = 995
● = 552	⊠ = (A) 3325 (B) 307 (C) 3023 (D) 703
◉ = 703	▨ = 554

Making Instructions:

Stitch embroidery where indicated referring to chart. Fold back the allowance all around twice, mitering at corners (refer to page 95), steady with slip st.

Napkin:

You'll Need (for 4 pieces):

· Fabric . . . Indian cloth (10 cm of fabric = 52 square meshes) 90 cm square White.

· Threads . . . D.M.C 6-strand embroidery floss:
3½ skeins of Plum (554); 1½ skeins each of Brilliant Green (703), Plum (552), Lemon Yellow (307); 1 skein each of Royal Blue (995), Beige (3023) and Azure Blue (3325); ½ skein of Emerald Green (910).

Finished Size: 38 cm square

Size of Stitch: 1 square of design = 1 square mesh of fabric

Making Instructions:

Referring to the design on luncheon mat, match center of fabric to that of flower, stitch embroidery with 3 strands. Finish raw edge in same manner as for luncheon mat.

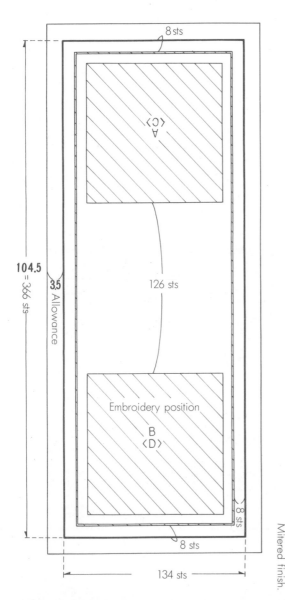

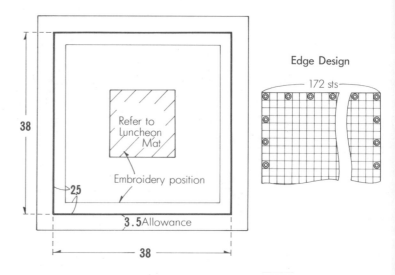

Edge Design

FRAMED PICTURE   shown on page 8

You'll Need:

· Fabric . . . Java cloth (10 cm of fabric = 35 square meshes) 45 cm by 52 cm Cream.

· Threads . . . D.M.C 6-strand embroidery floss:
3 skeins of Raspberry Red (3689); 2 skeins each of Emerald Green (911), Geranium Red (350, 352); 1½ skeins of Morocco Red (761); 1 skein each of Moss Green (471), Turkey Red (321), Geranium Red (349); ½ skein each of Scarlet (815, 304), Geranium Red (948), Cardinal Red

(347) and Moss Green (937, 469, 470, 472).

· Fittings . . . Frame Gold (background Navy Blue) 48.5 cm by 40.7 cm outmost of the frame.

Finished Size: 37.5 cm by 30 cm (decorated fabric)

Size of Stitch: 1 square of design = 1 square mesh of fabric

Making Instructions:

Stitch embroidery matching center of fabric to that of design. Fix the decorated piece in frame.

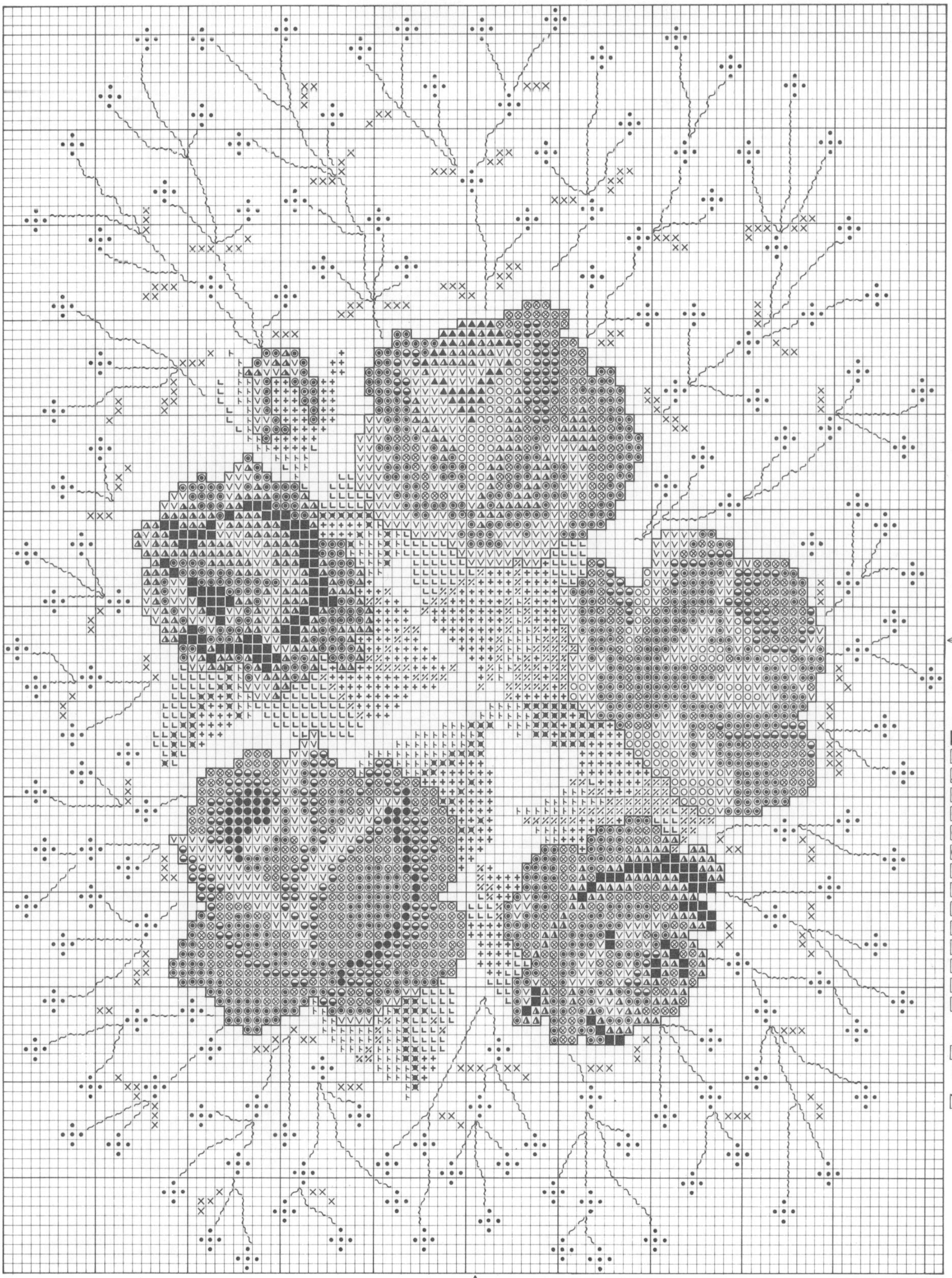

← Center

↑
Center

With 6 strands unless specified.

■ = 815
▲ = 304
△ = 321
● = 347
◒ = 349
⊗ = 350
◎ = 352
V = 761
O = 948
▣ = 937
☒ = 469
L = 470
+ = 471
⊢ = 472
• = 3689

4 strands
☒ = 911

Holbein stitch = 911

PIANO THROW shown on pages 8 — 9

You'll Need:

- Fabric . . . Java cloth (10 cm of fabric = 35 square meshes) 91 cm by 220 cm Beige.
- Threads . . . D.M.C 6-strand embroidery floss: 12½ skeins of Myrtle Grey (924); 10 skeins of Myrtle Grey (926); 9 skeins of Myrtle Grey (927); 8½ skeins of Garnet Red (326); 7½ skeins of Geranium Red (817); 7 skeins of Scarlet (498); 6 skeins of Morocco Red (761); 5 skeins of Old Rose (3350, 3354); 4½ skeins of Moss Green (937); 4 skeins of Red Brown (918); 3½ skeins of Pistachio Green (319); 2 skeins each of Light Yellow (3078), Copper Green (830); 1 skein each of Sepia (3371) and Red Brown (920); ½ skein of Golden Yellow (782, 783).

Finished Size: 217.5 cm by 90 cm

Size of Stitch: 1 square of design = 1 square mesh of fabric

Making Instructions:

Match center of fabric to that of design, stitch embroidery caring direction of A flower on both sides. Having stitched whole the design, finish three sides with buttonhole st.

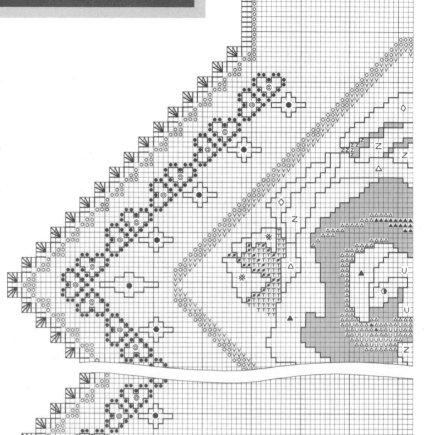

Buttonhole stitch

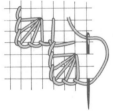

Having stitched, cut away the surplus right along the stitch.

With 6 strands

⊡ = 927	▨ = 830	z = 3350	◿ = 782
● = 924	T = 319	◑ = 783	L = 918
◎ = 817	△ = 761	U = 3078	✕ = 920
V = 926	▲ = 498	⊤ = 3371	
✖ = 937	◇ = 3354	▨ = 326	

190 = 665 sts

Selvage

86 sts
48 sts
45 sts
5 sts
90 = 314 sts
45 sts
5 sts
45 sts
5 sts
78 sts
1

A
B
C

4
23
6.5
7.5
16
3.5
8.5
20
6
9
9

Cut off after
the buttonhole st.

5 sts
5 sts
5 sts
48 sts
78 sts
45 sts
45 sts
217.5 = 761 sts

A
B

Buttonhole
stitch
(926)

C

Center

PILLOW

shown on pages 10 — 11

You'll Need:

- Fabric . . . Java cloth (10 cm of fabric = 35 square meshes) 90 cm by 47 cm each of Black for left, White for right.
- Threads . . . D.M.C 6-strand embroidery floss:
  (Left) 3 skeins each of White, Cornflower Blue (794); 2½ skeins each of Antique Blue (931), Ash Grey (318); 2 skeins of Seagull Grey (451); 1 skein each of Seagull Grey (452) and Ash Grey (415).

(Right) 3 skeins each of Black (310), Ash Grey (317); 2½ skeins of Ash Grey (414, 318); 2 skeins of Seagull Grey (451); 1 skein each of Seagull Grey (452) and Ash Grey (415).

- Fittings (for 1 portion) . . . 45 cm square inner case stuffed with kapok. 38 cm long zip fastener.

Finished Size: 43 cm square

Size of Stitch: 1 square of design = 1 square mesh of fabric

With 6 strands, ⟨ ⟩fof left and ( ) for right   ⊡=⟨White⟩(310)   ●=⟨931⟩(414)   ☒=⟨318⟩(318)   ⊠=⟨794⟩(317)   △=⟨451⟩(451)   ⊥=⟨452⟩(452)   Ⅰ=⟨415⟩(415)

Center

Making Instructions:

Cut fabric referring to chart, stitch embroidery matching center of fabric to that of design. Sew zip on back side, put on front right sides together, seam along the edge, turn right side out. Stuff kapok.

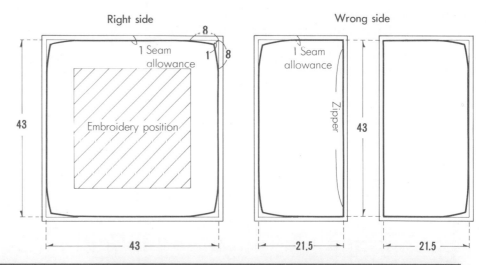

Right side

8
1
8

1 Seam allowance

Embroidery position

43

43

Wrong side

1 Seam allowance

Zipper

43

21.5

21.5

PANEL   shown on page 12

Above
You'll Need:
- Fabric . . . Java cloth (10 cm of fabric = 26 square meshes) 50 cm square Yellow.
- Threads . . . D.M.C 6-strand embroidery floss:
6 skeins each of Violet Mauve (327), Indigo (939); 4½ skeins of Copper Green (830); 3 skeins each of Peacock Blue (807) and White.

Finished Size: 42 cm square

Size of Stitch: 1 square of design = 1 square mesh of fabric

Making Instructions:
Match center of fabric to that of design, stitch embroidery symmetrically in all directions, arranging A & B alternately as shown on the chart. Have it finish at its specialty store.

Center→

With 6 strands

■ = 939
Ⓞ = White
☒ = 807
N = 830
● = 327

Ⓐ   Ⓑ

↑
Center

Below
You'll Need:
- Fabric . . . Java cloth (10 cm of fabric = 26 square meshes) 44 cm square Cream.
- Threads . . . D.M.C 6-strand embroidery floss:
1 skein each of Smoke Grey (640), Moss Green (934, 469), Scarab Green (3347), Copper Green (830), Pistachio Green (368); ½ skein each of Pistachio Green (319, 367),

Emerald Green (912), Sepia (3371), Cerise (601), Tangerine Yellow (740), Copper Green (834), Episcopal Purple (917), Brilliant Green (702, 704), Laurel Green (986), Moss Green (471); small amount each of Buttercup Yellow (444), Cerise (600), Soft Pink (819), Tangerine Yellow (741), Geranium Red (948), Beige (3047), Raspberry Red (3688), Pistachio Green (320), Emerald Green (955), Forget-me-not Blue (824, 828), Sevres Blue (798) and White.

51

Finished Size: 35.5 cm square
Size of Stitch: 1 square of design = 1 square mesh of fabric
Making Instructions:

Stitch embroidery matching center of fabric to that of design. Have it finish at its specialty store.

With 6 strands

■ = 3371	✗ = 912	⊿ = 3688	Ⓢ = 367
✗ = 444	⊗ = 955	⭕ = White	∅ = 469
◑ = 601	⊝ = 319	▲ = 824	● = 934
Ⓩ = 604	✚ = 368	T = 798	Y = 320
╱ = 819	⬗ = 986	• = 828	
Ⓛ = 740	⊹ = 702	✖ = 3347	
⊖ = 741	Λ = 3047	∩ = 640	
△ = 948	Ⓘ = 834	▨ = 471	
◧ = 830	◉ = 917	◎ = 704	

Center →

↑
Center

PILLOW   shown on page 13

You'll Need:
- Fabrics . . . Java cloth (10 cm of fabric = 35 square meshes) 35 cm square Beige, suede cloth 90 cm by 30 cm Brown, Emmy cloth 47 cm by 44 cm Beige.
- Threads . . . D.M.C 6-strand embroidery floss: 2 skeins of Umber (435); 1½ skeins each of Coffee Brown (898) and Moss Green (469); 1 skein of Tangerine Yellow (740); small amount of Canary Yellow (972).
- Fittings . . . 45 cm square inner case stuffed with kapok. 36 cm long zip fastener.

Finished Size: Refer to chart.

Size of Stitch: 1 square of design = 1 square mesh of fabric

Making Instructions:
Cut out pieces from fabric, match center of Java cloth to that of design, stitch embroidery symmetrically in all directions. Seam referring to chart, stuff kapok in shape.

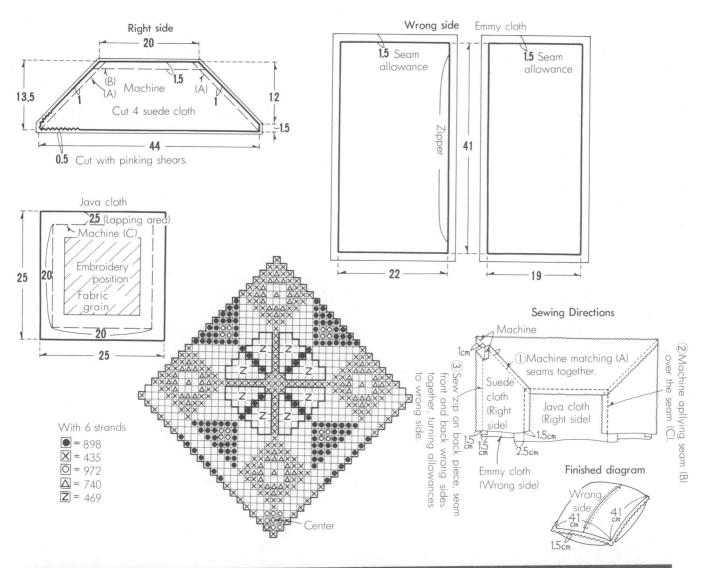

Right side

20

13.5

(B) (A) Machine (A)

1.5

1   1   12

1.5

Cut 4 suede cloth

44

0.5 Cut with pinking shears.

Wrong side   Emmy cloth

1.5 Seam allowance

1.5 Seam allowance

Zipper

41

22   19

Java cloth

2.5 (Lapping area)

Machine (C)

Embroidery position

Fabric grain

25   20   20

25

With 6 strands
- ● = 898
- ✕ = 435
- ◎ = 972
- △ = 740
- Z = 469

Center

Sewing Directions

Machine

1cm

①Machine matching (A) seams together.

②Machine applying seam (B) over the seam (C).

③Sew zip on back piece, seam front and back wrong sides together, turning allowances to wrong side.

Suede cloth (Right side)

Java cloth (Right side)

1.5cm   1.5   1.5   2.5cm

Emmy cloth (Wrong side)

Finished diagram

Wrong side   41 cm   41 cm

1.5cm

TABLECLOTH   shown on pages 14 — 15

You'll Need:
- Fabric . . . Java cloth (10 cm of fabric = 26 square meshes) 92 cm by 347 cm Beige.
- Threads . . . D.M.C 6-strand embroidery floss: 65 skeins of Indigo (322).

Finished Size: 163.5 cm by 135 cm

Size of Stitch: 1 square of design = 1 square mesh of fabric

Making Instructions:
Seam pieces together, match center of fabric to that of design, stitch design symmetrically in all directions with 9 strands. Fold back cut edge twice, mitering at corners (refer to page 93), slip st steady.

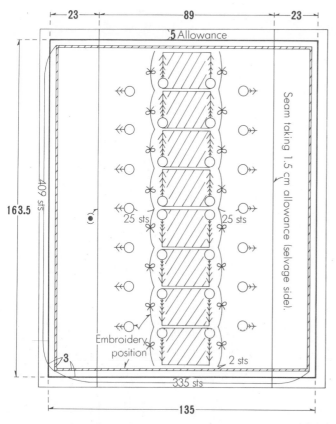

23 89 23

.5 Allowance

163.5

409 sts

25 sts   25 sts

Embroidery position

3

335 sts

2 sts

135

Seam taking 1.5 cm allowance (selvage side).

Edge Pattern:

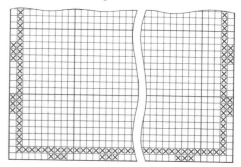

Finishing Allowance:

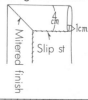

4 cm

1cm

Mitered finish

Slip st

Center

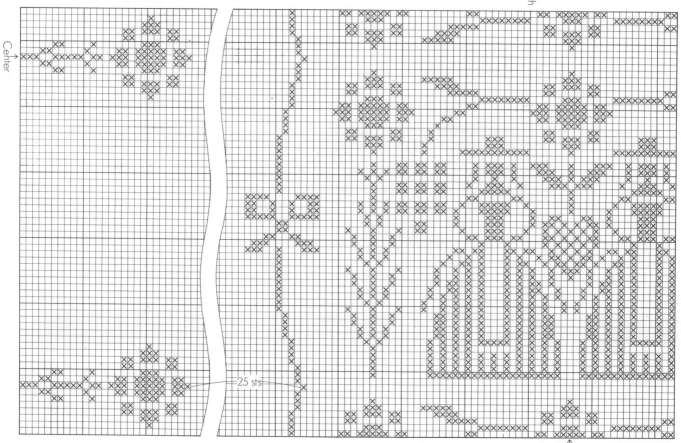

25 sts

Center

54

RUNNER

shown on page 16

You'll Need:

- Fabric . . . Java cloth (10 cm of fabric = 35 square meshes) 37 cm by 125 cm Beige.
- Threads . . . D.M.C 6-strand embroidery floss: 4 skeins each of Parma Violet (208), Plum (554); 3½ skeins of Pistachio Green (320, 368); 2 skeins each of Plum (553), Pistachio Green (367), Umber (435); 1½ skeins of Scarab Green (3347); 1 skein of Saffron (725, 727); ½ skein each of Umber (436) and Beige Brown (841); small amount of Terra-cotta (356).

Finished Size: 118 cm by 30 cm

Size of Stitch: 1 square of design = 1 square mesh of fabric

Making Instructions:

Match center of fabric to that of design, stitch embroidery where indicated. Turn cut edge all around twice to wrong side, mitering at corners (refer to page 95), slip st steady.

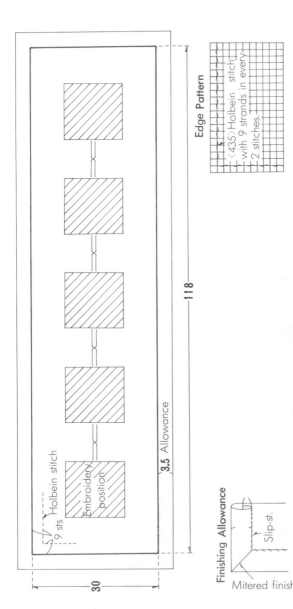

Edge Pattern

<435> Holbein stitch with 9 strands in every 2 stitches.

Holbein stitch

9 sts

Embroidery position

118

3.5 Allowance

30

Finishing Allowance

Slip-st.

Mitered finish

With 6 strands

| T = 553 |
| V = 208 |
| Z = 368 |
| ◉ = 320 |
| ◁ = 320 |
| ◬ = 554 |
| X = 356 |
| L = 725 |
| ○ = 727 |
| ● = 367 |
| S = 3347 |
| ✕ = 436 |
| ╱ = 841 |

Center

Center

PILLOW shown on pages 18 – 19

You'll Need:
- Fabric (for 1 portion) . . . Java cloth (10 cm of fabric = 35 square meshes) 91 cm by 44 cm Beige.
- Threads . . . D.M.C 6-strand embroidery floss:
  (Left) 3 skeins of Azure Blue (3325); 1 skein each of Flame Red (606), Moss Green (469), Green (3053); ½ skein each of Mahogany (400), Emerald Green (909), Turkey Red (321) and Myrtle Grey (926).
  (Right) 3 skeins of Myrtle Grey (924); 1 skein each of Moss Green (469), Green (3053), Saffron (725); ½ skein each of Mahogany (400), Emerald Green (909) and Turkey Red (321).
- Fittings (for 1 portion) . . . 1.8 cm wide braid 180 cm long Red for left, Gold Brown for right. 40 cm long zip fastener. 45 cm square inner case stuffed with kapok.

Finished Size: 44 cm square
Size of Stitch: 1 square of design = 1 square mesh of fabric
Making Instructions:
Stitch embroidery on center piece front. Seam referring to chart.

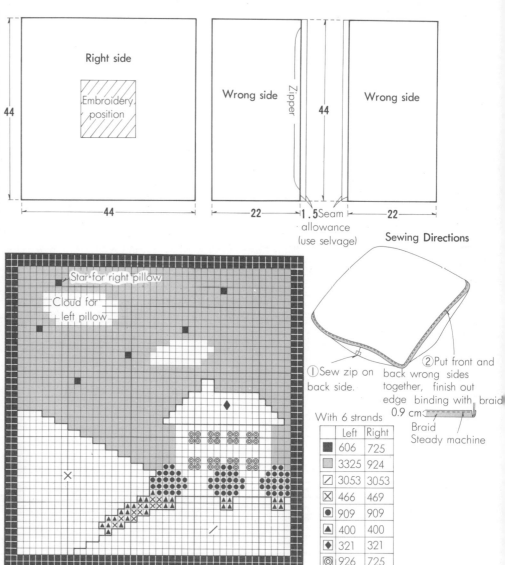

Right side

Embroidery position

44

44

Wrong side   Zipper   Wrong side

22   1.5 Seam allowance (use selvage)   22

Sewing Directions

① Sew zip on back side. ② Put front and back wrong sides together, finish out edge binding with braid 0.9 cm
Braid
Steady machine

Star for right pillow.
Cloud for left pillow

With 6 strands

	Left	Right
■	606	725
▧	3325	924
▨	3053	3053
✕	466	469
●	909	909
▲	400	400
◆	321	321
◎	926	725

FRAMED PICTURE shown on page 10

You'll Need:
- Fabric . . . Indian cloth (10 cm of fabric = 52 square meshes) 38 cm by 32 cm Beige.
- Threads . . . D.M.C 6-strand embroidery floss:
  1 skein each of Sky Blue (747), White; ½ skein of Mahogany (402); small amount each of Sepia (3371), Peacock Green (991), Emerald Green (911), Royal Blue (796, 995, 996), Smoke Grey (640, 822), Flame Red (606, 608), Garnet Red (326, 335), Ash Grey (762), Drab (610, 612), Beige Brown (841), Hazel-nut Brown (422), Umber (738), Cream (746), Scarlet (815, 498), Tangerine Yellow (743), Red Brown (922), Umber Gold (977), Chestnut (407, 950), Sevres Blue (798), Indigo (334), Forget-me-not Blue (824, 809), Poppy (666), Saffron (725), Dark Brown (3033), Antique Blue (930), Peacock Blue (806, 807) and Black (310).
- Fittings . . . Frame (29.3 cm by 23.2 cm inside).

Finished Size: 21.5 cm by 17.5 cm (decorated fabric)
Size of Stitch: 1 square of design = 1 square mesh of fabric
Making Insturctions:
Stitch embroidery matching center of fabric to that of design. Having stitched whole design, fix in frame.

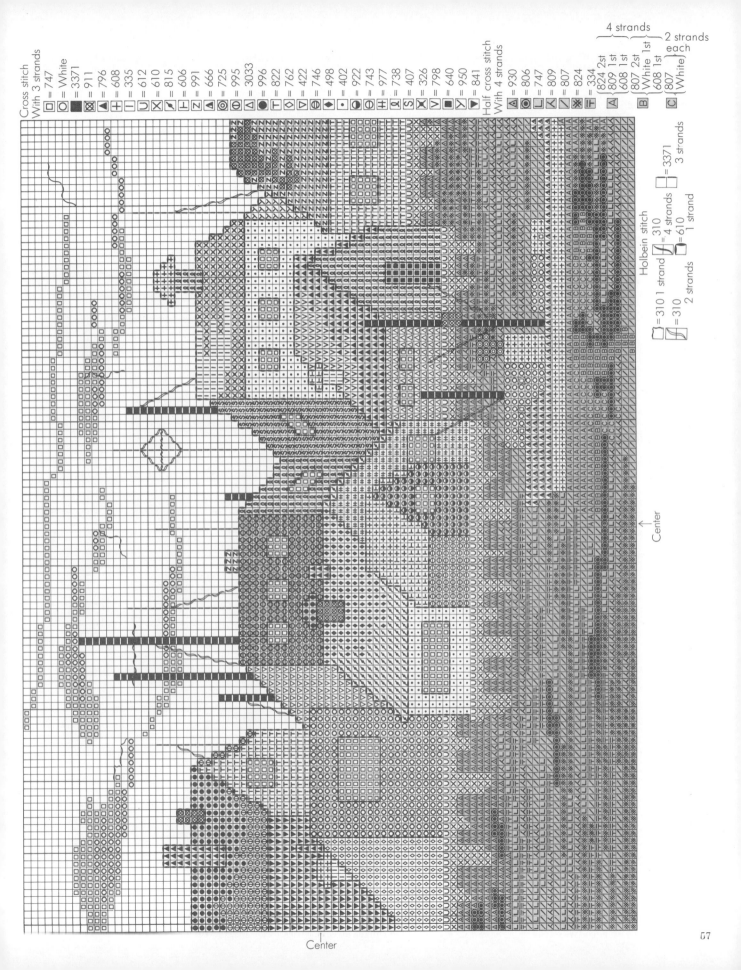

You'll Need:
- Fabric . . . Java cloth (10 cm of fabric = 35 square meshes) 45 cm by 95 cm Beige.
- Threads . . . D.M.C 6-strand embroidery floss:
  1 skein each of Brilliant Green (704), Emerald Green (911), Smoke Grey (640); ½ skein each of Yellow Green (733), Copper Green (833), Forget-me-mot Blue (809); small amount each of Cerise (601, 603, 604), Drab (610), Canary Yellow (972), Tangerine Yellow (740), Geranium Red (754), Sevres Blue (798) and White.

Finished Size: 40 cm by 34.5 cm
Size of Stitch: 1 square of design = 1 square mesh of fabric
Making Instructions:
  Stitch embroidery where indicated, have it finish at its specialty store.

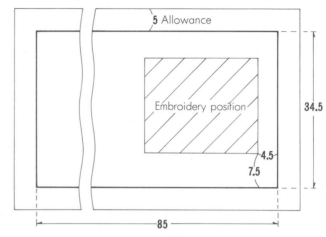

With 6 strands   ☐=704 ☒=733 ▲=911 ∅=833 ☐=640 ■=601 ●=610 ✳=972 ☒=603
☒=740 △=754 V=798 ☒=604 ∕= ☐=809 Holbein stitch ☐=640
White

PANEL shown on page 23

Above

You'll Need:

- Fabric . . . Indian cloth (10 cm of fabric = 52 square meshes) 18 cm square Blue.
- Threads . . . D.M.C 6-strand embroidery floss:

  floss:

  small amount each of Raspberry Red (3685, 3688), Episcopal Purple (718), Violet Mauve (327), Parma Violet (208), Moss Green (469, 470), Yellow Green (732), Copper Green (831), Drab (610), Umber (433), Sevres Blue (798) and Beige (3047).

Finished Size: 12 cm square

Size of Stitch: 1 square of design = 1 square mesh of fabric

Making Instructions:

Stitch embroidery matching center of fabric to that of design. Have it finish in panel at its specialty store.

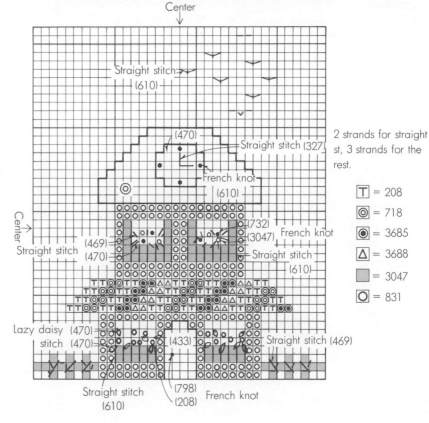

2 strands for straight st, 3 strands for the rest.

- ⊤ = 208
- ◎ = 718
- ◉ = 3685
- △ = 3688
- ▦ = 3047
- Ο = 831

Below

You'll Need:

- Fabric . . . Indian cloth (10 cm of fabric = 52 square meshes) 18 cm square Olive.
- Threads . . . D.M.C 6-strand embroidery floss:

  small amount each of Moss Green (469, 470, 471), Raspberry Red (3685), Episcopal Purple (718), Dark Brown (3033), Umber (435, 739), Copper Green (830), Yellow Green (733, 734), Parma Violet (208), Coffee Brown (898) and Sevres Blue (799).

Finished Size: 12 cm square

Size of Stitch: 1 square of design = 1 square mesh of fabric

Making Instructions:

Stitch embroidery matching center of fabric to that of design. Have it finish in panel at its specialty store.

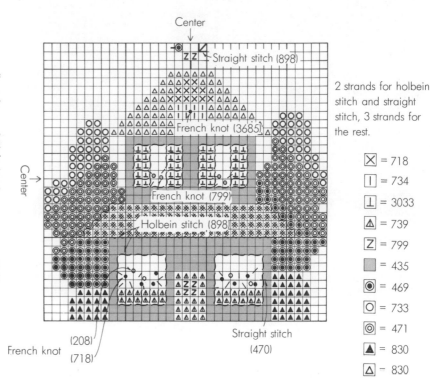

2 strands for holbein stitch and straight stitch, 3 strands for the rest.

- ✕ = 718
- | = 734
- ⊥ = 3033
- △ = 739
- Z = 799
- ▦ = 435
- ◉ = 469
- Ο = 733
- ◎ = 471
- ▲ = 830
- △ = 830
- ✳ = 470

59

CENTER PIECE shown on page 20

You'll Need:
- Fabric . . . Java cloth (10 cm of fabric = 35 square meshes) 56 cm square Beige.
- Threads . . . D.M.C 6-strand embroidery floss:
  3½ skeins of drab (611); 3 skeins each of Canary Yellow (972), Brilliant Green (704); 1½ skeins each of Emerald Green (911), Cerise (601), Episcopal Purple (718), Laurel Green (988), Plum (552); 1 skein each of Yellow Green (734) and Beige (3022); ½ skein of Copper Green (833).

Finished Size: 49.5 cm square

Size of Stitch: 1 square of design = 1 square mesh of fabric

Making Instructions

Match center of fabric to that of design, stitch embroidery where indicated.

Turn cut edge twice to wrong side mitering at each corner (refer to page 95), slip st steady.

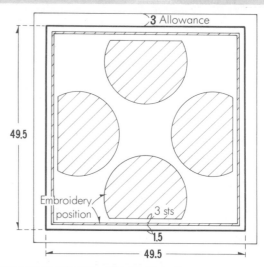

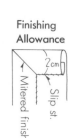

Finishing Allowance

Center

With 6 strands

X	= 911
⊙	= 988
O	= 704
△	= 972
V	= 3022
L	= 718
U	= 833
⊘	= 552
●	= 611
⊘	= 734
—	= 601

Edge Pattern

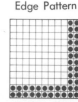

CENTER PIECE shown on page 21

You'll Need:
- Fabric . . . Indian cloth (10 cm of fabric = 52 square meshes) 57 cm square White.
- Threads . . . D.M.C 6-strand embroidery floss:
  3½ skeins of Ash Grey (318); 2½ skeins of Parma Violet (211); 2 skeins each of Ash Grey (414), Laurel Green (986), Pistachio Green (368), Saffron (727); 1½ skeins of Ash Grey (415); 1 skein each of White, Scarab Green (3347), Sevres Blue (800), Plum (554), Soft Pink (818), Raspberry Red (3688), ½ skein each of Ash Grey (762), Saffron (725), Forget-me-not Blue (825), Sevres Blue (799), Indigo (939), Cerise (602, 604), Raspberry Red (3685); small amount each of Violet Mauve (327), Parma Violet (208) and Scarlet (814).

Finished Size: 51 cm square

Size of Stitch: 1 square of design = 1 square mesh of fabric

Making Instructions:

Match center of fabric to that of design, stitch whole the design referring to chart.

Turn cut edge twice to wrong side, mitering at each corner (refer to page 95), steady with slip st.

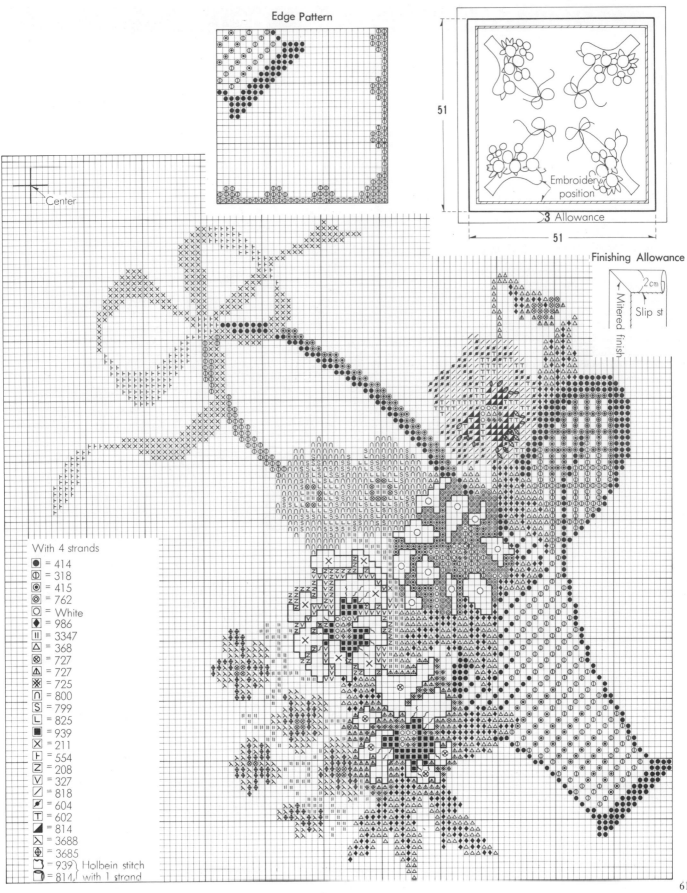

Edge Pattern

51

51

Embroidery position

3 Allowance

Finishing Allowance

2 cm

Slip st

Mitered finish

Center

With 4 strands

●	= 414
⏀	= 318
◉	= 415
◎	= 762
O	= White
◆	= 986
‖	= 3347
△	= 368
⊗	= 727
◮	= 727
✖	= 725
∩	= 800
S	= 799
L	= 825
■	= 939
X	= 211
F	= 554
Z	= 208
V	= 327
╱	= 818
◪	= 604
T	= 602
◣	= 814
⋋	= 3688
⊕	= 3685
◠	= 939 } Holbein stitch
◡	= 814 } with 1 strand

Above

You'll Need:

- Fabric . . . Indian cloth (10 cm of fabric = 52 square meshes) 23 cm square White.
- Threads . . . D.M.C 6-strand embroidery floss:
  1½ skeins of Beige Brown (842); small amount each of Brilliant Green (701, 704), Moss Green (935), Black (310), Umber (433), Poppy (666), Cerise (603), Plum (552), Seagull Grey (451), Geranium Red (948), Royal Blue (996) and Copper Green (833).
- Fittings . . . Frame 15 cm square inside Red.

Finished Size: Same size as frame.

Size of Stitch: 1 square of design = 1 square mesh of fabric

Making Instructions:

Stitch embroidery matching center of fabric to that of design. Having worked embroidery, fix frame.

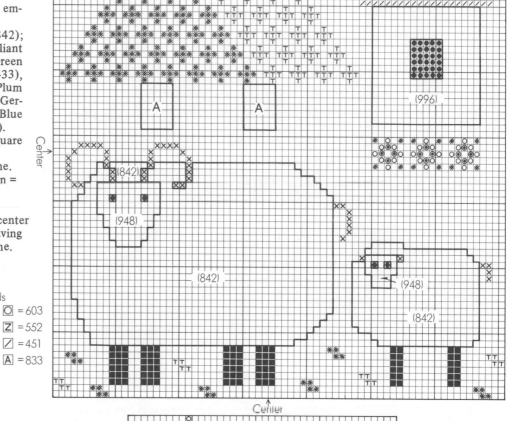

With 4 strands

T	= 704	O	= 603
✖	= 701	Z	= 552
■	= 935	∕	= 451
◉	= 310	A	= 833
✕	= 433		
◎	= 666		

Below

You'll Need:

- Fabric . . . Indian cloth (10 cm of fabric = 52 square meshes) 18 cm square Red.
- Threads . . . D.M.C 6-strand embroidery floss:
  small amount each of Indigo (336), Royal Blue (796, 995), Plum (552), Peony Rose (956), Canary Yellow (973), Flame Red (608) and White.
- Fittings . . . Frame 15 cm square inside Red.

Finished Size: Same size as frame.

Size of Stitch: 1 square of design = 1 square mesh of fabric

Making Instructions:

Stitch embroidery matching center of fabric to that of design. Having worked embroidery, fix in frame.

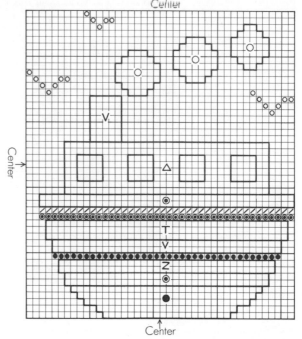

With 4 strands

●	= 336
◎	= 796
Z	= 552
V	= 956
T	= 995
△	= 973
∕	= 608
O	= White

COASTER shown on page 24

You'll Need:
- Fabrics (for 1 piece) . . . Indian cloth (10 cm of fabric = 52 square meshes) 12.5 cm square Beige. Unbleached sheeting 12.5 cm square.
- Threads . . . D.M.C 6-strand embroidery floss:

(A) small amount each of Peony Rose (957), Emerald Green (912), Saffron (727), Forget-me-not Blue (809), Umber (435), Umber Gold (977), Brilliant Green (704), Canary Yellow (973), Magenta Rose (962) and Black (310).

(B) small amount each of Tangerine Yellow (743), Emerald Green (912), Umber Gold (977), Umber (435), Forget-me-not Blue (826, 809), Geranium Red (351), Beaver Grey (645) and Black (310).

(C) small amount each of Emerald Green (912), Forget-me-not Blue (809), Peony Rose (957), Saffron (727), Umber (435), Umber Gold (977), Brilliant Green (704), Magenta Rose (962), Canary Yellow (973) and Black (310).

(D) small amount each of Forget-me-not Blue (826, 809), Tangerine Yellow (743), Umber Gold (977), Umber (435), Emerald Green (954), Geranium Red (351), Beaver Grey (645) and Black (310).

(E) small amount each of Tangerine Yellow (743), Peony Rose (957), Forget-me-not Blue (809), Emerald Green (954), Umber (435), Umber Gold (977), Brilliant Green (704), Magenta Rose (962), Canary Yellow (973) and Black (310).

- Fittings (for each) . . . 1.2 cm wide Gray Brown bias tape 42 cm long.

Finished Size: 12.5 cm in diameter
Size of Stitch: 1 square of design = 1 square mesh of fabric
Making Instructions:

Match center of fabric to that of design, stitch embroidery. Put front and back wrong sides together, bind out edge into 0.6 cm wide piping with bias tape.

A、C、E

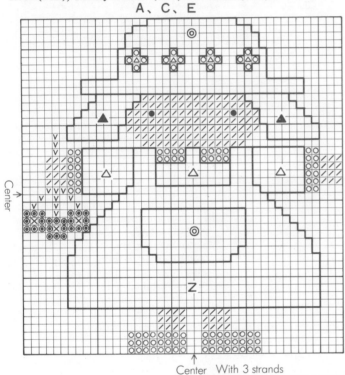

B、D

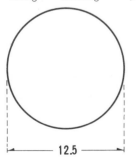

Top piece···Indian cloth ⎫ Cut 1
Lining······Sheeting ⎭ each

12.5

With 3 strands

	A	C	E
◎	912	809	957
○	727	957	809
△	809	727	954
▲	435	435	435
∕	977	977	977
●	310	310	310
V	704	704	704
◉	973	962	962
✕	962	973	973
Z	957	912	743

With 3 strands

	B	D
△	912	743
∕	977	977
●	310	310
▲	435	435
✕	809	954
■	645	645
Z	743	809
◖	826	826
◎	351	351

63

Napkin
You'll Need: (for 1 piece):
- Fabric . . . Java cloth (10 cm of fabric = 35 square meshes) 44 cm square White.
- Threads . . . D.M.C 6-strand embroidery floss:
  2 skeins of Fire Red (900).

Finished Size: 39.5 cm square

Size of Stitch: 1 square of design = 1 square mesh of fabric

Making Instructions:
Stitch embroidery where indicated with 6 strands. Turn allowance twice to wrong side, mitering at each corner (refer to page 95), slip st steady.

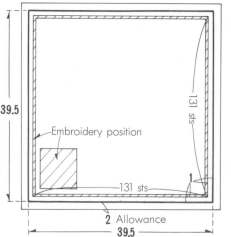

Embroidery position

131 sts

131 sts

39.5

39.5

2 Allowance

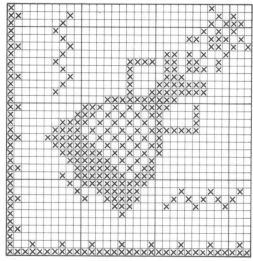

Tea Cozy
You'll Need:
- Fabrics . . . Java cloth (10 cm of fabric = 35 square meshes) 80 cm by 42 cm White. Cotton for lining 80 cm by 35 cm.
- Threads . . . D.M.C 6-strand embroidery floss:
  2 skeins of Fire Red (900).
- Fittings . . . 1.8 cm wide Red bias tape 120 cm long. Batting.

Finished Size: Refer to chart.

Size of Stitch: 1 square of design = 1 square mesh of fabric

Making Instructions:
Stitch embroidery on front piece where indicated with 6 strands. Having finished embroidery, sew referring to chart.

Luncheon Mat
You'll Need (for 1 piece):
- Fabric . . . Java cloth (10 cm of fabric = 35 square meshes) 44 cm by 35 cm White.
- Threads . . . D.M.C 6-strand embroidery floss:
  3 skeins of Fire Red (900).

Finished Size: 39.5 cm by 30.5 cm

Size of Stitch: 1 square of design = 1 square mesh of fabric

Making Instructions:
Match center of fabric to that of design, stitch embroidery with 6 strands. Having stitched whole the design, turn the allowance all around twice to wrong side, mitering at each corner (refer to page 95), slip st steady.

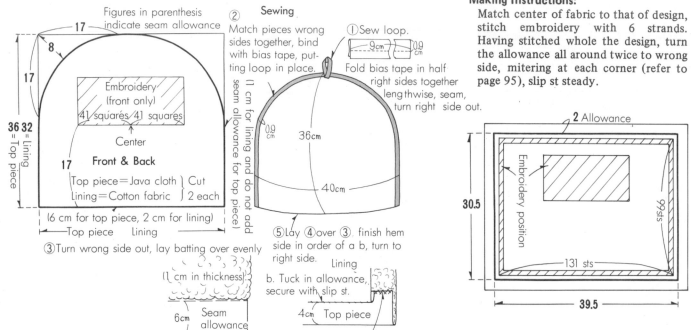

Figures in parenthesis indicate seam allowance

17
8
17
17

36 = lining 32 = Top piece

Embroidery
(front only)
41 squares / 41 squares
Center

Front & Back

17

Top piece = Java cloth ⎱ Cut
Lining = Cotton fabric ⎰ 2 each

(6 cm for top piece, 2 cm for lining)
Top piece   Lining

③Turn wrong side out, lay batting over evenly

(1 cm in thickness)

6cm   Seam allowance

④Sew lining right sides together, turn right side out.

(1 cm for lining and do not add seam allowance for top piece)

② **Sewing**

Match pieces wrong sides together, bind with bias tape, putting loop in place.

①Sew loop.
9cm   0.9 cm

Fold bias tape in half right sides together lengthwise, seam, turn right side out.

0.9 cm

36cm

40cm

⑤Lay ④ over ③, finish hem side in order of a b, turn to right side.

Lining

b. Tuck in allowance, secure with slip st.

4cm   Top piece

a. Turn up allowance, secure with herringbone st.

2 Allowance

Embroidery position

30.5

99 sts

131 sts

39.5

Center of luncheon mat

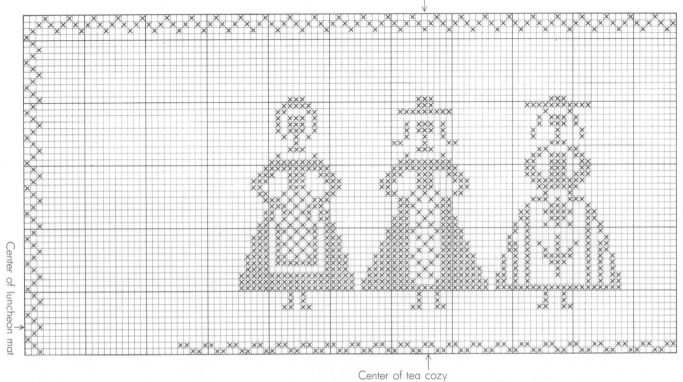

Center of luncheon mat

Center of tea cozy

CAP OF JAM JAR & LABEL shown on page 24

You'll Need:
- Fabrics (for 1 pair) . . . Indian cloth (10 cm of fabric = 52 square meshes) 28 cm by 13 cm White. Cotton for lining 28 cm by 13 cm.
- Threads . . . D.M.C 6-strand embroidery floss:
  Left – small amount each of Soft Pink (899), Tangerine Yellow (743), Sevres Blue (799), Brilliant Green (703) and Umber (433).
  Center – small amount each of Poppy (666), Flame Red (606), Tangerine Yellow (742), Brilliant Green (704) and Coffee Brown (898).
  Right – small amount each of Geranium Pink (891), Cornflower Blue (793), Brilliant Green (702), Buttercup Yellow (444) and Moss Green (934).
- Fittings . . . 1.2 cm wide bias tape Pink for left, Gold Yellow for middle, Blue for right 150 cm long each. Elastic 18 cm.

Finished Size: Refer to chart.

Size of Stitch: 1 square of design = 1 square mesh of fabric

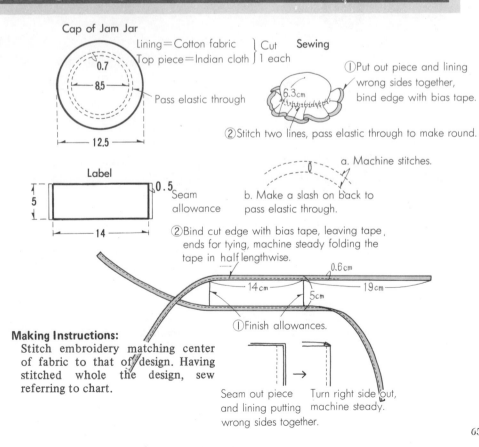

Cap of Jam Jar

Lining = Cotton fabric } Cut
Top piece = Indian cloth } 1 each

0.7
8.5
12.5
Pass elastic through

Label
5
0.5
14
Seam allowance

Sewing

①Put out piece and lining wrong sides together, bind edge with bias tape.

6.3cm

②Stitch two lines, pass elastic through to make round.

a. Machine stitches.

b. Make a slash on back to pass elastic through.

②Bind cut edge with bias tape, leaving tape ends for tying, machine steady folding the tape in half lengthwise.

0.6 cm
14 cm
19 cm
5cm

①Finish allowances.

Seam out piece and lining putting wrong sides together.

Turn right side out, machine steady.

Making Instructions:
Stitch embroidery matching center of fabric to that of design. Having stitched whole the design, sew referring to chart.

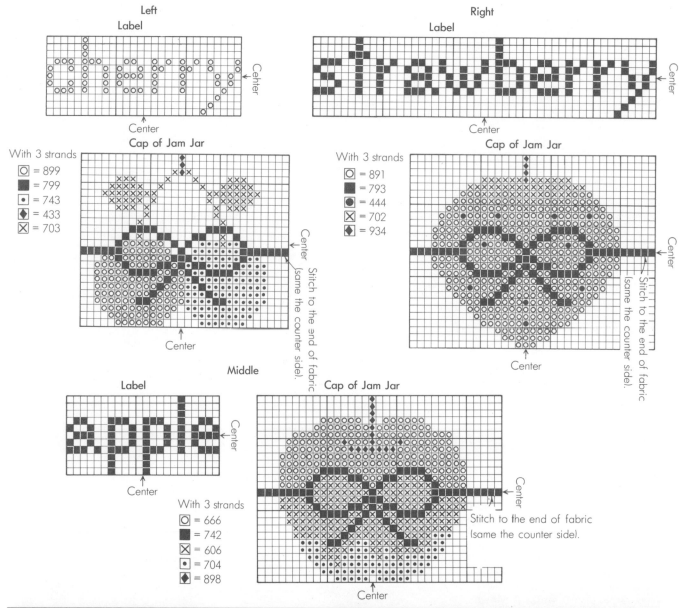

Left Label

Right Label

Cap of Jam Jar

With 3 strands
- ☐ = 899
- ■ = 799
- ● = 743
- ◆ = 433
- ✕ = 703

With 3 strands
- ☐ = 891
- ■ = 793
- ● = 444
- ✕ = 702
- ◆ = 934

Cap of Jam Jar

Center

Center

Stitch to the end of fabric (same the counter side).

Middle

Label

Center

Cap of Jam Jar

With 3 strands
- ☐ = 666
- ■ = 742
- ✕ = 606
- ● = 704
- ◆ = 898

Center

Center

Stitch to the end of fabric (same the counter side).

TRAY MAT   *shown on page 25*

You'll Need:
- Fabrics . . . Indian cloth (10 cm of fabric = 52 square meshes) 42 cm by 27 cm White Green. Unbleached sheeting 42 cm by 27 cm.
- Threads . . . D.M.C 6-strand embroidery floss:
1½ skeins of Emerald Green (912); small amount each of Geranium Red (351, 352), Emerald Green (909), Golden Yellow (780), Saffron (725, 727), Tangerine Yellow (741), Turkey Red (321), Raspberry Red (3688), Peony Rose (957), Antique Blue (930), Copper Green (831), Canary Yellow (973), Plum (552), Royal Blue (797), Forget-me-not Blue (826), Azure Blue (3325), Brilliant Green (704)

and Coffee Brown (898).
- Fittings . . . 1.2 cm wide Light Green bias tape 141 cm long.

Finished Size: 41.5 cm by 26.5 cm

Size of Stitch: 1 square of design = 1 square mesh of fabric

Making Instructions:
Match center of fabric to that of design, stitch arranging design symmetrically referring to chart. Match to lining right sides out, bind cut edge with bias tape.

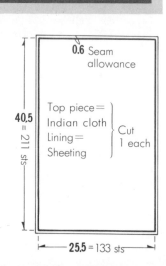

0.6 Seam allowance

40.5 = 211 sts

Top piece = Indian cloth Lining = Sheeting   } Cut 1 each

25.5 = 133 sts

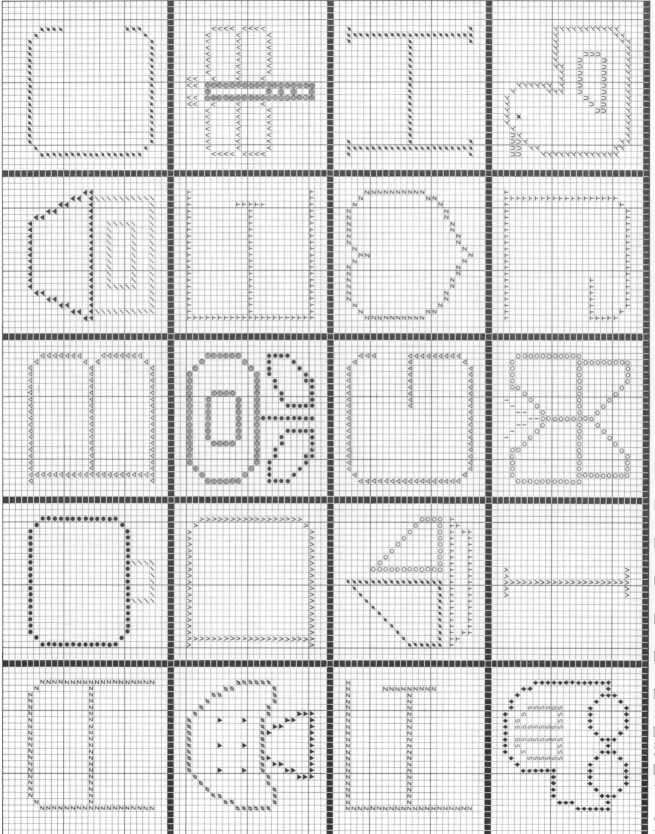

With 3 strands Z=351 ●=909 Z=780 A=725 A=552 V=741 T=3688 O=957 Z=321 Z=826 ◆=797 S=3325 I=704 A=930 A=973 U=727 X=352 X=898 ■=912

⟨Center→

67

FRAMED PICTURE
shown on pages 30 – 31

You'll Need:

- Fabric (for 1 piece) . . . Java cloth (10 cm of fabric = 26 square meshes) 43 cm by 39 cm Beige.
- Threads . . . D.M.C 6-strand embroidery floss:
  Left – 2 skeins of Geranium Red (892); 1½ skeins each of Cerise (604), Peacock Green (992, 993); 1 skein each of Sevres Blue (799), Canary Yellow (971), Cerise (602), Indigo (311); ½ skein each of Parma Violet (208), Peony Rose (957); small amount each of Geranium Red (754), Lemon Yellow (307), Ash Grey (318), Antique Blue (930, 932), Plum (552), Parma Violet (209), Turkey Red (321), Soft Pink (899), Peony Rose (956), Royal Blue (796), Episcopal Purple (718), Fire Red (947), Sevres Blue (798), Scarab Green (3347), Poppy (666), Flame Red (606) and White.

Left

Center →

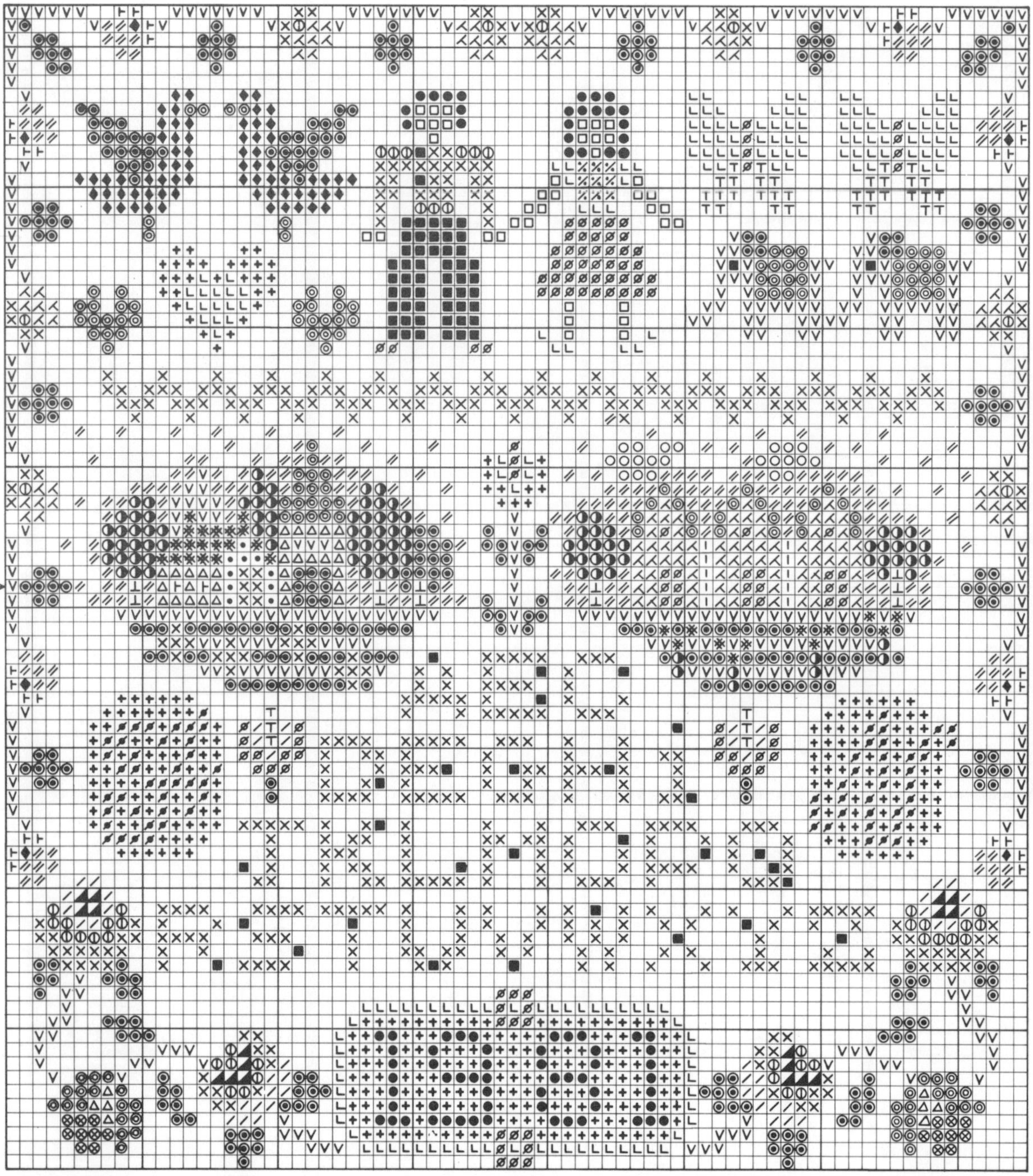

With 6 strands

◎ = 971
● = 930
◐ = 3347
% = 899
⊗ = 947
◢ = 321
□ = 754
△ = 307
☒ = 892
I = 209
V = 993
Φ = 666
✳ = 606
◉ = 992
■ = 311
⊥ = 932
/ = 956
// = 799
T = 718
L = 602
⊢ = 798
∠ = 957
ø = 208
◆ = 796
○ = White
+ = 604
ø = 552
• = 318

Right — 2 skeins of Geranium Red (892); 1 skein each of Soft Pink (899), Parma Violet (208), Peacock Green (993), Cerise (602), Canary Yellow (971); ½ skein each of Peacock Green (991), Flame Red (606); small amount each of Sevres Blue (799), Royal Blue (796, 996), Antique Blue (930, 932), Fire Red (946), Cerise (604), Parma Violet (209), Indigo (311), Geranium Red (754), Brilliant Green (703), Emerald Green (910), Peacock Green (992), Umber (433) and White.
· Fittings . . . Frame (35 cm by 31 cm inside).

Finished Size: Same size as frame.
Size of Stitch: 1 square of design = 1 square mesh of fabric
Making Instructions:
Work embroidery matching center of fabric to that of design. Having stitched whole the design, fix in frame.

Right

With 6 strands

X	= 892
▲	= 799
▨	= 899
■	= 930
V	= 433
✖	= 796
◑	= 208
✐	= 946
⋋	= 971
T	= 606
◎	= 992
⊕	= 996
∅	= 604
U	= 209
●	= 311
□	= 754
O	= White
◐	= 993
◉	= 991
⊗	= 910
Z	= 602
‖	= 932
L	= 703
◣	= 930

Holbein stitch

69

A

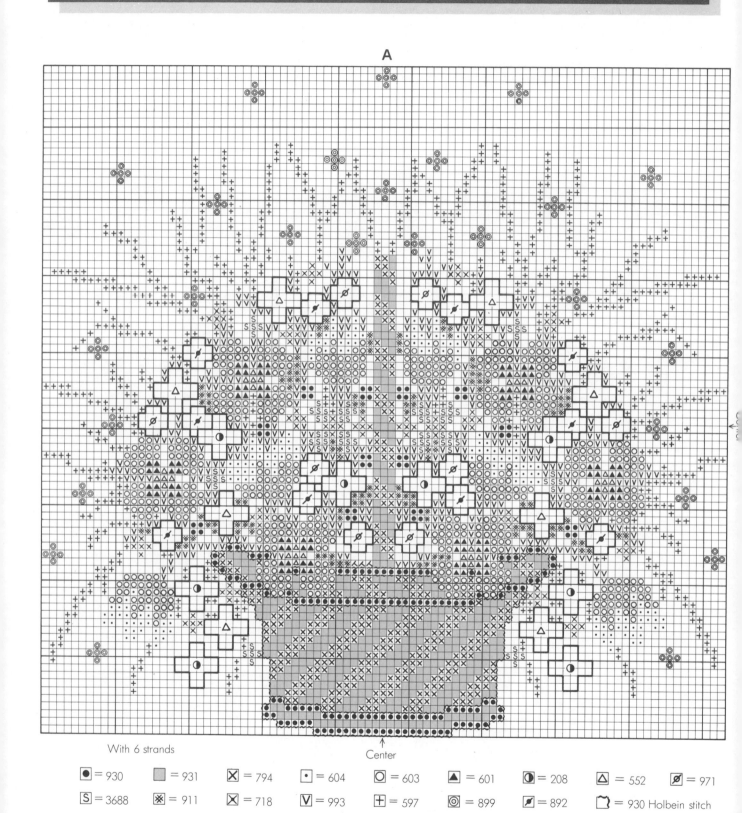

With 6 strands

● = 930   ▨ = 931   ✖ = 794   ⊡ = 604   ◯ = 603   ▲ = 601   ◐ = 208   △ = 552   ∅ = 971

S = 3688   ✳ = 911   ✗ = 718   V = 993   ✚ = 597   ◎ = 899   ⬥ = 892   ⬡ = 930 Holbein stitch

Center

B

With 6 strands

Center

● = 930	▩ = 931	⋏ = 932	▲ = 601	⊡ = 604	⊙ = 603	△ = 552	◐ = 208	⊠ = 718	S = 3688
⊞ = 597	V = 993	✳ = 911	Z = 995	∩ = 996	▲ = 799	⊗ = 704	✎ = 892	∅ = 971

You'll Need:

- Fabrics . . . Java cloth (10 cm of fabric = 25 square meshes) 90 cm by 420 cm Beige. Indian cloth (10 cm of fabric = 52 square meshes) 90 cm by 220 cm Dark Blue. Cotton for lining 90 cm by 400 cm.
- Threads . . . D.M.C 6-strand embroidery floss:
  12 skeins of Greenish Grey (597); 9 skeins of Cerise (603); 6½ skeins each of Peacock Green (993), Antique Blue (930, 931); 4 skeins each of Cornflower Blue (794), Parma Violet (208); 3½ skeins each of Cerise (601, 604), Emerald Green (911), Plum (552); 3 skeins each of Geranium Red (892), Episcopal Purple (718), Canary Yellow (971), Sevres Blue (799); 2½ skeins each of Raspberry Red (3688), Soft Pink (899); 1 skein each of Royal Blue (995, 996), Antique Blue (932) and Brilliant Green (704).
- Fittings . . . 1.2 cm wide bias tape White 570 cm long. 7 cm wide cotton lace White 843 cm long.

Finished Size: refer to chart.

Size of Stitch: 1 square of design = 1 square mesh of fabric

Making Instructions:

Match center of motif to that of design, embroider 4 pieces each of A, B. Having stitched all motifs, sew referring to chart.

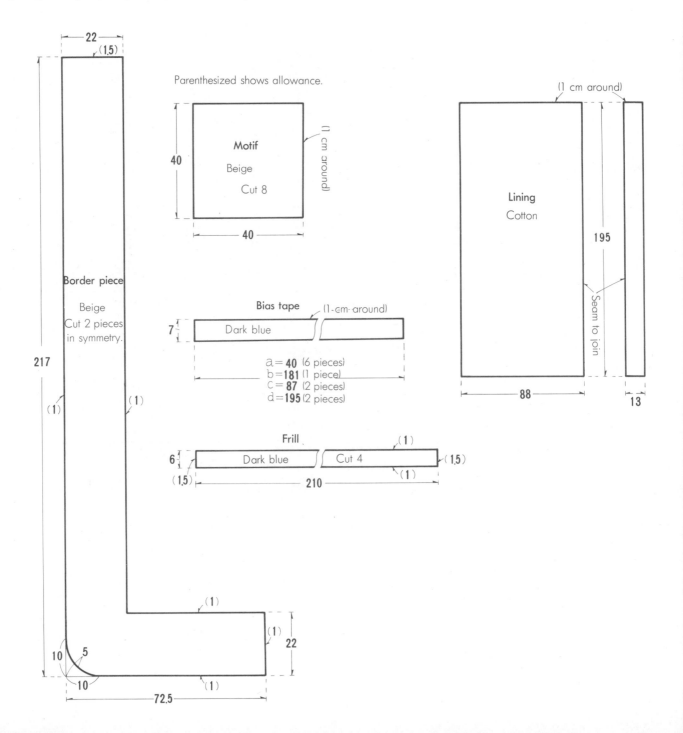

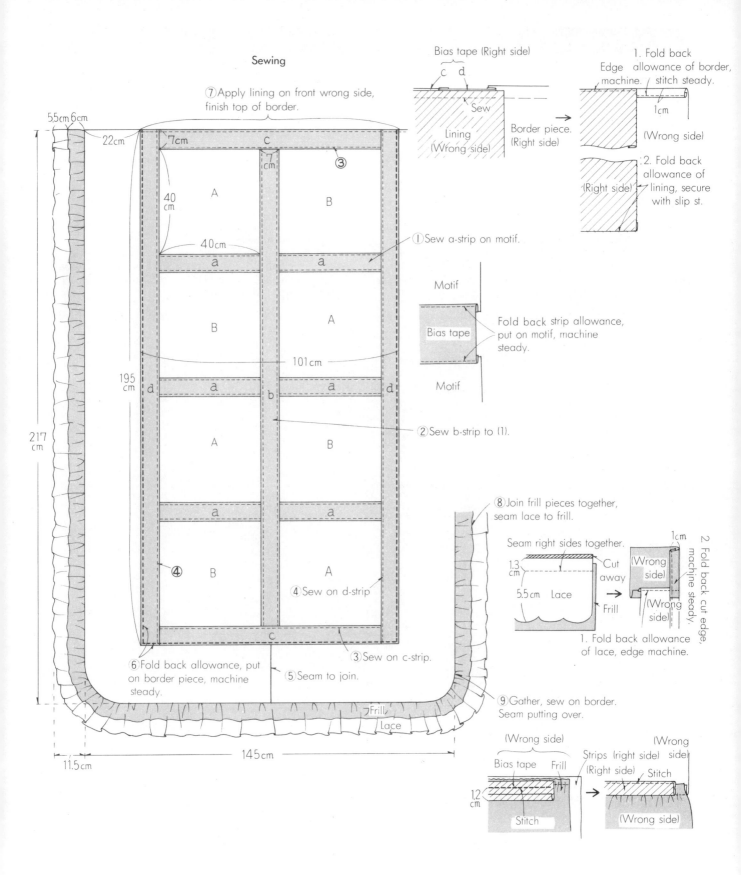

Sewing

⑦Apply lining on front wrong side, finish top of border.

Bias tape (Right side)

c   d

Sew

Lining (Wrong side)

Border piece. (Right side)

1. Fold back
Edge   allowance of border,
machine.   stitch steady.

1cm

(Wrong side)

:2. Fold back allowance of lining, secure with slip st.

(Right side)

5.5cm 6cm

22cm

7cm

c

7cm

③

A   B

40 cm

40cm

a   a

①Sew a-strip on motif.

Motif

Bias tape

Fold back strip allowance, put on motif, machine steady.

Motif

B   A

101cm

195 cm

d   a   a   b   a   a   d

②Sew b-strip to (1).

217 cm

A   B

B   A

④

④Sew on d-strip

a   a

c

⑧Join frill pieces together, seam lace to frill.

Seam right sides together.

1cm

1.3 cm

Cut away

(Wrong side)

5.5 cm   Lace

Frill

2 Fold back cut edge, machine steady.

(Wrong side)

1. Fold back allowance of lace, edge machine.

⑥Fold back allowance, put on border piece, machine steady.

⑤Seam to join.

③Sew on c-strip.

⑨Gather, sew on border. Seam putting over.

Frill

Lace

(Wrong side)

Bias tape   Frill

Strips (right side)

(Right side)

(Wrong side)

Stitch

1.2 cm

Stitch

(Wrong side)

145cm

11.5cm

You'll Need:

- Fabric . . . Indian cloth (10 cm of fabric = 52 square meshes) Pink for A, White Green for B, Blue for C, Dark Yellow for D, Light Brown for E 22 cm by 12 cm each.
- Threads . . . D.M.C 6-strand embroidery floss:

(A) small amount each of Cerise (604), Umber (433, 739), Sevres Blue (800), Saffron (725), Buttercup Yellow (444), Scarlet (498), Episcopal Purple (915), Turkey Red (321), Royal Blue (820), Peacock Green (991), Plum (550) and Coffee Brown (938).

(B) small amount each of Brilliant Green (701), Saffron (727), Geranium Red (892, 948), Umber (436), Tangerine Yellow (740), Coffee Brown (938) and Scarlet (498).

(C) small amount each of Peony Rose (956), Scarlet (498), Soft Pink (819), White, Tangerine Yellow (743), Umber (436), Umber Gold (975), Royal Blue (996), Forget-me-not Blue (825) and Parrakeet Green (904).

(D) small amount each of Raspberry Red (3688), Soft Pink (818), Emerald Green (954), Scarlet (498), White, Parma Violet (211), Umber (433, 436), Coffee Brown (938), Peacock Green (991) and Royal Blue (820).

(E) small amount each of Royal Blue (796), Flame Red (606), Soft Pink (818), Greenish Grey (598), Coffee Brown (938), Umber Gold (975), Raspberry Red (3688) and Scarlet (498).

- Fittings . . . 0.3 cm diameter string Dark Red for A, B, D, Navy Blue for C, E 42 cm long each. Cotton batting.

Finished Size: 10 cm square

Size of Stitch: 1 square of design = 1 square mesh of fabric

Making Instructions:

Stitch embroidery matching center of front to that of design. Seam right sides together, leaving its opening, turn right side out. Stuff batting, sew opening closed, apply string in position.

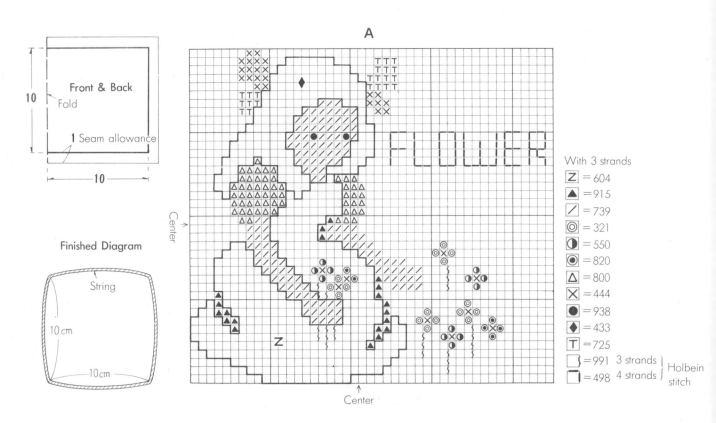

Finished Diagram

"Finish Raw Edge Before Stitching"

It is essential to oversew the raw edges of fabric pieces (especially the fabrics suitable for cross st) so that the handling of works becomes very smooth.

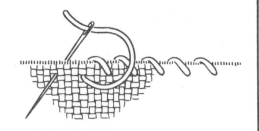

B·E

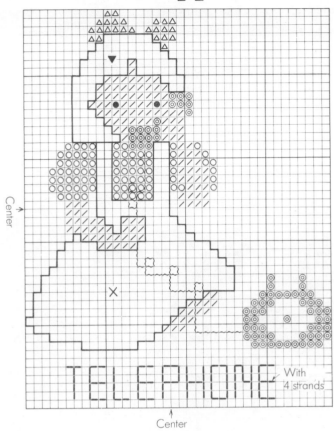

Use 3 strands of embroidery thread unless specified.

	B	E
◉	892	606
⁄	948	818
✕	701	796
○	727	598
●	938	938
▼	436	975
△	740	3688

Holbein stitch

	B	E
▢	498	498
⬠	892	606

With 4 strands

C·D

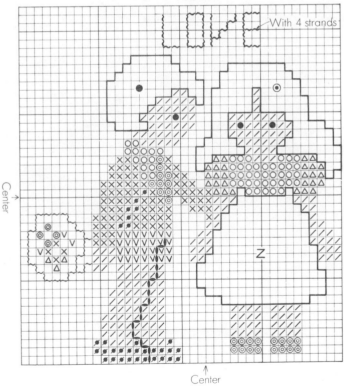

With 4 strands

Use 3 strands of embroidery thread unless specified.

	C	D
◉	498	498
⁄	819	818
Z	956	3688
○	White	White
△	743	211
⊙	436	433
●	975	938
✕	996	954
⬗	825	991
V	904	820

Holbein stitch

	C	D
⬠	498	498
⬠	825	991
⬠	436	436

You'll Need:
- Fabric . . . Java cloth (10 cm of fabric = 35 square meshes) 45 cm by 95 cm Beige.
- Threads . . . D.M.C 6-strand embroidery floss: 1½ skeins each of Garnet Red (326), Dull Mauve (778); 1 skein of Soft Pink (818), ½ skein each of Golden Yellow (783), Cerise (602), Sevres Blue (800); small amount each of Umber (433, 436), Umber Gold (975), Tangerine Yellow (743), Parrakeet Green (904), Scarab Green (3347), Peacock Green (991), Raspberry Red (3688, 3689), Cerise (604), Ash Grey (415), Royal Blue (820, 996), Sevres Blue (799) and Black (310).

With 6 strands

⊠ = 778	■ = 326	O = 818	⊠ = 433	⊡ = 436	⊘ = 975	⊘ = 783	⊠ = 743	◆ = 904	◇ = 3347	▽ = 991	⦿ = 602
◉ = 3688	⊚ = 3689	+ = 800	⊖ = 604	⊠ = 415	▲ = 310	∩ = 996	⊝ = 820	S = 799	Holbein stitch ⤲ = 3347		

Finished Size: 40 cm by 34.5 cm
Size of Stitch: 1 square of design = 1 square mesh of fabric
Making Instructions:
 Embroider where indicated, have it finish at the specialty
 store.

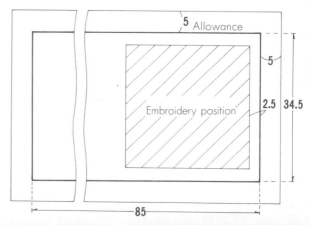

SPECTACLE CASE & VANITY CASE & PEN CASE & BOX JACKET

shown on page 34

Spectacle Case

You'll Need:

· Fabrics . . . Indian cloth (10
 cm of fabric = 52 square
 meshes) 20 cm by 12 cm
 Pink. Cotton for lining 20
 cm square.
· Threads . . . D.M.C 6-strand
 embroidery floss:
 small amount each of Cerise
 (600), Turkey Red (321),
 Soft Pink (899), Mahogany
 (300), Plum (552), Parrakeet Green (904).
Finished Size: 9 cm in width
 18 cm in depth
Size of Stitch: 1 square of design = 1 square mesh of fabric
Making Instructions:
 Stitch embroidery on front
 where indicated. Having
 stitched whole the design
 sew referring to chart.

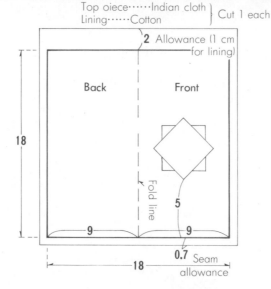

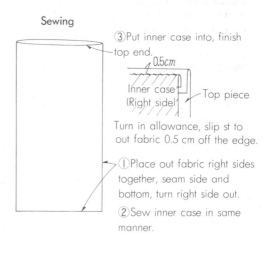

③Put inner case into, finish
 top end.

Turn in allowance, slip st to
out fabric 0.5 cm off the edge.

①Place out fabric right sides
together, seam side and
bottom, turn right side out.

②Sew inner case in same
manner.

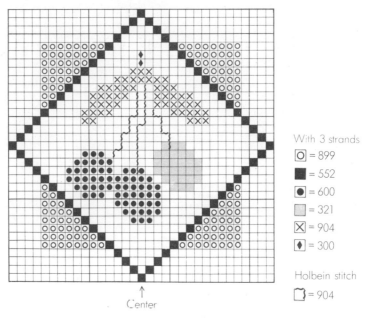

With 3 strands
☐ = 899
■ = 552
● = 600
▨ = 321
☒ = 904
◆ = 300

Holbein stitch
▱ = 904

Vanity Case

You'll Need:

- Fabrics . . . Indian cloth (10 cm of fabric = 52 cm square meshes) 30 cm by 20 cm Blue. Cotton for lining 30 cm by 20 cm.
- Threads . . . D.M.C 6-strand embroidery floss:
  small amount each of Sky Blue (518), Indigo (823), Cornflower Blue (792), Parma Violet (209) and White.
- Fittings . . . 1.2 cm wide bias tape Blue 40 cm long.

Finished Size: 14 cm in width 18 cm in depth

Size of Stitch: 1 square of design = 1 square mesh of fabric

Making Instructions:

Work embroidery matching center of fabric to that of design. Having stitched whole the design, sew referring to chart.

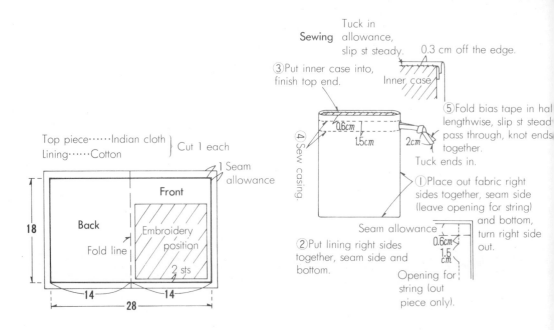

Sewing

① Place out fabric right sides together, seam side (leave opening for string) and bottom, turn right side out.

② Put lining right sides together, seam side and bottom.

③ Put inner case into, finish top end.

④ Sew casing.

⑤ Fold bias tape in half lengthwise, slip st steady, pass through, knot ends together. Tuck ends in.

Tuck in allowance, slip st steady.

0.3 cm off the edge.

Inner case

0.6cm 1.5cm 2cm

Seam allowance

Opening for string (out piece only).

0.6cm 1.5 cm

Top piece······Indian cloth
Lining······Cotton } Cut 1 each

1 Seam allowance

Front
Back
Embroidery position
Fold line
2 sts

18
14 14
28

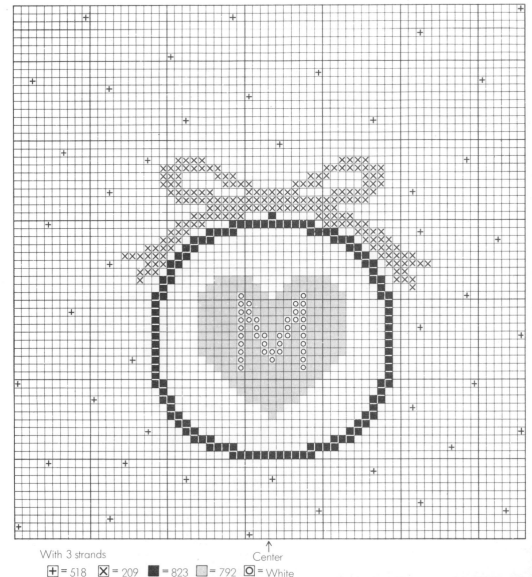

With 3 strands   Center

+ = 518   X = 209   ■ = 823   ▨ = 792   O = White

Pen Case

You'll Need:
- Fabrics . . . Indian cloth (10 cm of fabric = 52 square meshs) 21 cm by 23 cm Pink. Cotton for lining 21 cm by 23 cm.
- Threads . . . D.M.C 6-strand embroidery floss: small amount each of Cerise (600), Soft Pink (899) and Parma Violet (209).
- Fittings . . . 1 pair of snaps (mid in size).

Finished Size: 9 cm in width 18 cm in depth

Size of Stitch: 1 square of design = 1 square mesh of fabric

Making Instructions:
Work embroidery on front where indicated. Having stitched whole the design, make referring to chart.

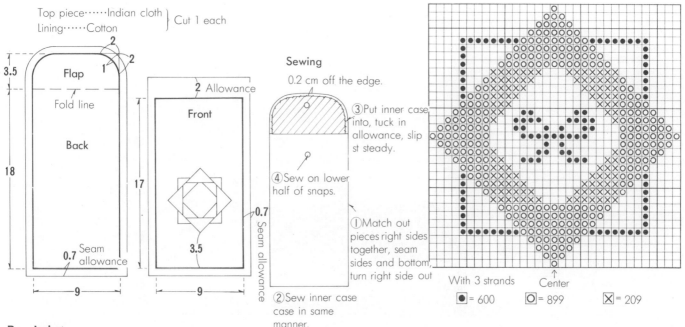

Box Jacket

You'll Need:
- Fabrics . . . Indian cloth (10 cm of fabric = 52 square meshs) 14 cm by 25 cm Pink. Cotton for lining 14 cm by 19 cm.
- Threads . . . D.M.C 6-strand embroidery floss: small amount each of Parrakeet Green (904), Soft Pink (899) and Cerise (600).

Finished Size: 13 cm by 9 cm

Size of Stitch: 1 square of design = 1 square mesh of fabric

Making Instructions:
Work embroidery on front where indicated. Having stitched whole the design, make referring to chart.

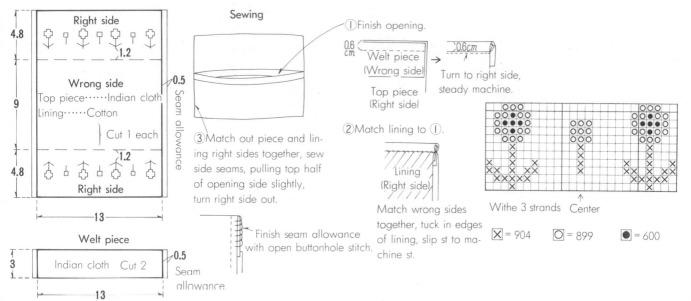

You'll Need:
- Fabrics (for 1 portion) . . . Indian cloth (10 cm of fabric = 52 square meshes) 16 cm by 40 cm Beige. Cotton for lining 16 cm by 40 cm. Broad Dark Brown for left, Olive Green for right 50 cm square each.
- Threads . . . D.M.C 6-strand embroidery floss:
  (Left) small amount each of Laurel Green (986), Parrakeet Green (904), Moss Green (471), Turkey Red (321), Soft Pink (899), Tangerine Yellow (743), Emerald Green (909), Sky Blue (518), Parma Violet (209), Umber Gold (975), Coffee Brown (938) and Cornflower Blue (792).
  (Right) small amount each of Parrakeet Green (904), Moss Green (471), Brilliant Green (699), Cerise (600), Red Brown (921), Golden Yellow (783), Umber Gold (976),

Copper Green (834), Beige Brown (842) and Coffee Brown (938).
- Fittings . . . (for left) 0.5 cm diameter Brown string 110 cm long. Pair of snaps (mid in size). (for right) 0.5 cm diameter twisted string Moss Green 110 cm long. 1 of 1.8 cm diameter button. Crochet hook size 4/0.

Finished Size: 16 cm in width 13.5 cm in depth
Size of Stitch: 1 square of design = 1 square mesh of fabric
Making Instructions:

Stitch embroidery where indicated. Having worked whole the design, make referring to chart.

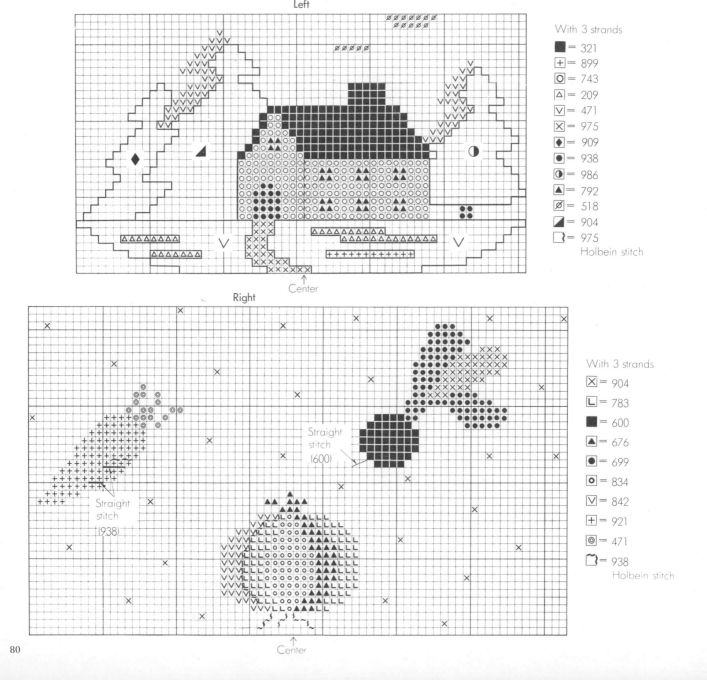

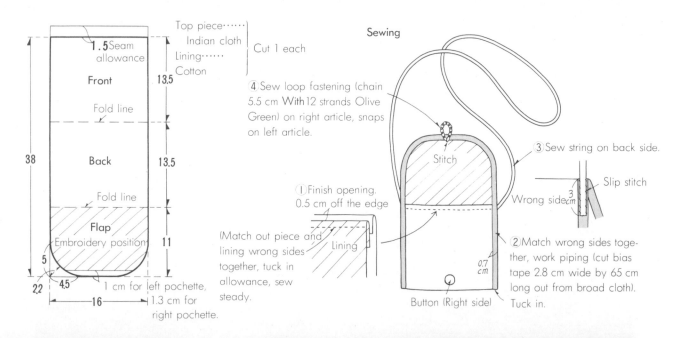

1.5 Seam allowance

Front

Fold line

Back

Fold line

Flap
Embroidery position

38

13.5

13.5

11

5

2.2 4.5 1 cm for left pochette,
16   1.3 cm for right pochette.

Top piece⋯⋯
Indian cloth   Cut 1 each
Lining⋯⋯
Cotton

Sewing

④Sew loop fastening (chain 5.5 cm With 12 strands Olive Green) on right article, snaps on left article.

Stitch

③Sew string on back side.

①Finish opening. 0.5 cm off the edge

Wrong side 3 cm   Slip stitch

(Match out piece and lining wrong sides together, tuck in allowance, sew steady.

Lining

②Match wrong sides together, work piping (cut bias tape 2.8 cm wide by 65 cm long out from broad cloth). Tuck in.

0.7 cm

Button (Right side)

PANEL shown on pages 36 — 37

Spring

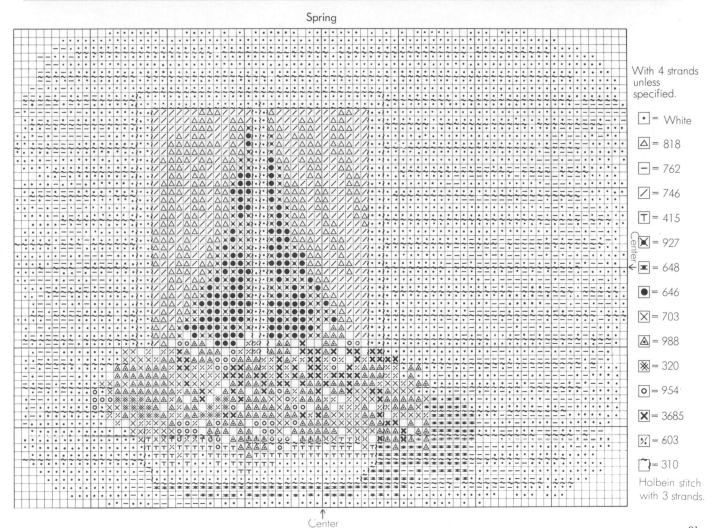

Center

With 4 strands unless specified.

⊡ = White

△ = 818

— = 762

∕ = 746

T = 415

▣ = 927

▣ = 648

● = 646

✕ = 703

△ = 988

▨ = 320

○ = 954

✕ = 3685

✕ = 603

⌐ = 310

Holbein stitch with 3 strands.

Center

You'll Need (for 1 piece):

- Fabrics . . . Congress (10 cm of fabric = 70 square meshes) 29 cm by 23 cm Beige. Cotton for lining 25 cm by 19 cm.
- Threads . . . D.M.C 6-strand embroidery floss:

Spring — 3 skeins of White; 1½ skeins of Ash Grey (762), ½ skein each of Cream (746), Soft Pink (818), Black (310); small amount each of Beaver Grey (646, 648), Ash Grey (415), Myrtle (927), Brilliant Green (703), Laurel Green (988), Pistachio Green (320), Emerald Green (954), Raspberry Red (3685) and Cerise (603).

Summer — 1½ skeins of Umber (738); 1 skein each of Umber (436), Moss Green (937); small amount each of Chestnut (950), Brilliant Green (702), Laurel Green (988), Dull Mauve (315), Mahogany (400), Beaver Grey (647), Myrtle Grey (928), Coffee Brown (898), Cornflower Blue (794) and Black (310).

Autumn — 2 skeins each of Copper Green (832), Saffron (727); 1 skein each of Ash Grey (318), Seagull Grey (452), Golden Yellow (780, 783), Canary Yellow (972); small amount each of Copper Green (830), Drab (610), Umber Gold (975), Azure Blue (775), Soft Pink (899), Greenish Grey (597), Beaver Grey (646) and Black (310).

Winter — 2 skeins of Indigo (312); 1 skein each of Cornflower Blue (792, 793), Indigo (322), Sevres Blue (798), Antique Blue (931); small amount each of Black (310), Copper Green (832), Lemon Yellow (445), Golden Yellow (782), Canary Yellow (972) and Peacock Green (993).

- Fittings . . . 2 of 1.5 cm diameter plastic ring. Board of styrenefoam (adhesive either side) 23 cm by 17 cm.

Finished Size: 23 cm by 17 cm

Size of Stitch: 1 square of design = 2 square mesh of fabric

Making Instructions:

Work embroidery matching center of fabric to that of design. Having stitched whole the design, make into panel.

Summer

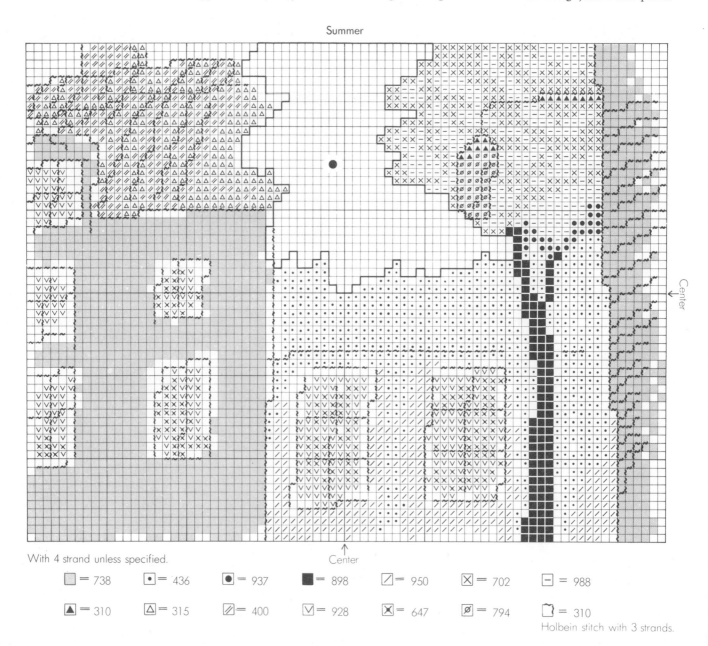

With 4 strand unless specified.

Center

☐ = 738	⊡ = 436	⦿ = 937	■ = 898	∕ = 950	☒ = 702	− = 988

▲ = 310	△ = 315	⬚ = 400	∨ = 928	☒ = 647	⦰ = 794	☐ = 310

Holbein stitch with 3 strands.

Sewing

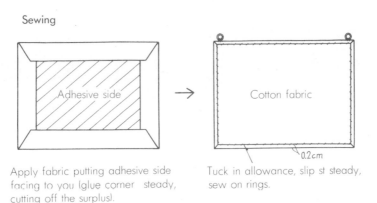

Apply fabric putting adhesive side facing to you (glue corner steady, cutting off the surplus).

Tuck in allowance, slip st steady, sew on rings.

0.2cm

Autumn

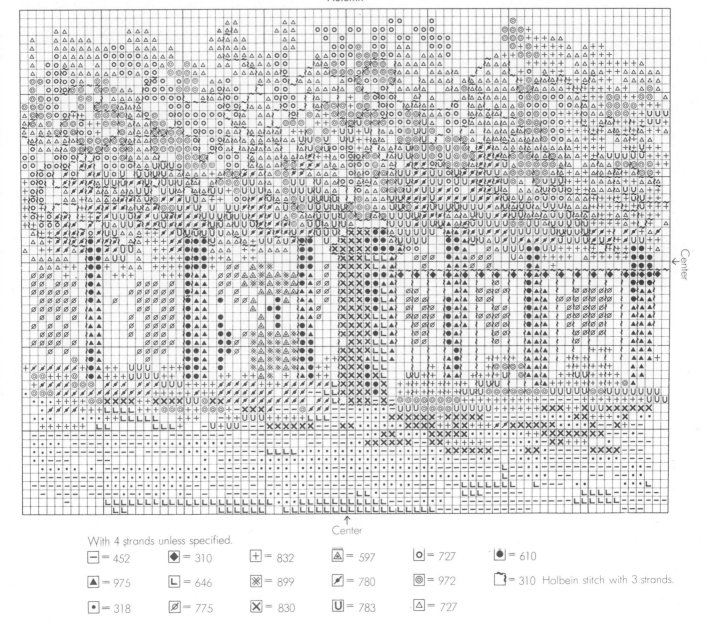

← Center

↑ Center

With 4 strands unless specified.

▬ = 452	◆ = 310	✚ = 832	△̲ = 597	○ = 727	◖ = 610
▲ = 975	L = 646	✖ = 899	⁄ = 780	◎ = 972	⌐ = 310 Holbein stitch with 3 strands.
⊡ = 318	Ø = 775	✕ = 830	U = 783	△ = 727	

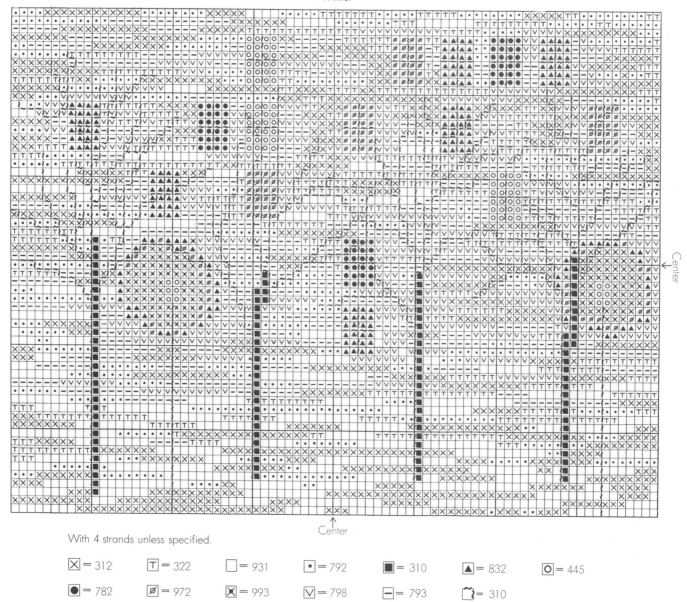

With 4 strands unless specified.

⊠ = 312	T = 322	☐ = 931	• = 792	■ = 310	▲ = 832	⊙ = 445
● = 782	∅ = 972	⊠ = 993	V = 798	— = 793	⬚ = 310	

Holbein stitch with 3 strands.

You'll Need:

· Fabric . . . Java cloth (10 cm of fabric = 35 square meshes) 73 cm by 23 cm Beige.
· Threads . . . D.M.C 6-strand embroidery floss:
1 skein of Scarab Green (3348), ½ skein of White; small amount each of Sevres Blue (798, 800), Plum (552), Parma Violet (209), Umber (435, 436), Soft Pink (818), Peony Rose (957), Geranium Red (352), Emerald Green (912, 954), Tangerine Yellow (743) and Ash Grey (762).

· Fittings . . . 0.3 cm diameter White string 80 cm long.
Finished Size: 20 cm in width 33 cm in depth
Size of Stitch: 1 square of design = 1 square mesh of fabric
Making Instructions:
Work embroidery on front, matching center of fabric to that of design. Having stitched whole the design, sew referring to chart.

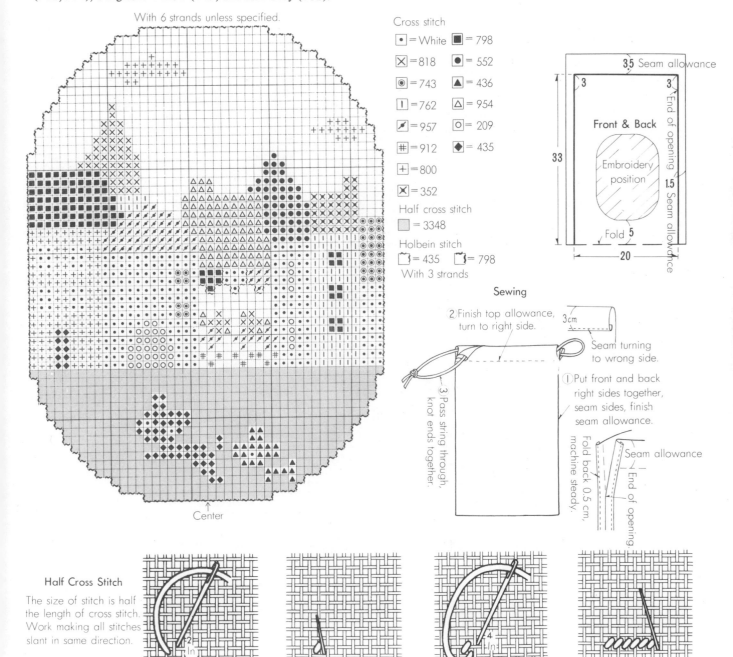

With 6 strands unless specified.

Center

Cross stitch

• = White	■ = 798		
✕ = 818	● = 552		
◉ = 743	▲ = 436		
❘ = 762	△ = 954		
✦ = 957	◯ = 209		
⊞ = 912	◆ = 435		
✛ = 800			
✗ = 352			

Half cross stitch
▨ = 3348

Holbein stitch
⌐ = 435 ⌐ = 798
With 3 strands

Front & Back

Embroidery position

Fold

3.5 Seam allowance
3   3
33
1.5
5
20
End of opening
Seam allowance

Sewing

②Finish top allowance, turn to right side.

3cm

Seam turning to wrong side.

①Put front and back right sides together, seam sides, finish seam allowance.

③Pass string through, knot ends together.

Fold back 0.5 cm, machine steady.

Seam allowance

End of opening

Half Cross Stitch

The size of stitch is half the length of cross stitch. Work making all stitches slant in same direction.

Bring needle out at 1, insert in 2.

Bring needle out at 3 (right below 2).

Insert needle in 4 (above right side).

You'll Need:

- Fabrics . . . Java cloth (10 cm of fabric = 35 square meshes) 27 cm by 33 cm Black. Cotton for lining 27 cm by 33 cm.
- Threads . . . D.M.C 6-strand embroidery floss: small amount each of Soft Pink (819), White, Geranium Pink (894), Peony Rose (957), Forget-me-not Blue (809), Sevres Blue (800), Magenta Rose (963), Pistachio Green (368), Moss Green (966) and Geranium Red (754).

- Fittings . . . 20 cm long zip fastener.

Finished Size: Refer to chart.

Size of Stitch: 1 square of design = 1 square mesh of fabric

Making Instructions:

Embroider design on front where indicated. Having stitched whole the design, sew referring to chart.

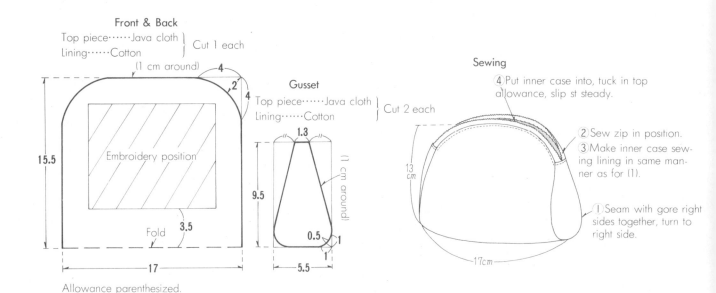

Front & Back
Top piece······Java cloth
Lining······Cotton } Cut 1 each
(1 cm around)

4
2
4

15.5

Embroidery position

Fold

3.5

17

Allowance parenthesized.

Gusset
Top piece······Java cloth
Lining······Cotton } Cut 2 each

1.3
9.5
(1 cm around)
0.5   1
1
5.5

Sewing

④ Put inner case into, tuck in top allowance, slip st steady.

② Sew zip in position.

③ Make inner case sewing lining in same manner as for ①.

① Seam with gore right sides together, turn to right side.

13 cm

17cm

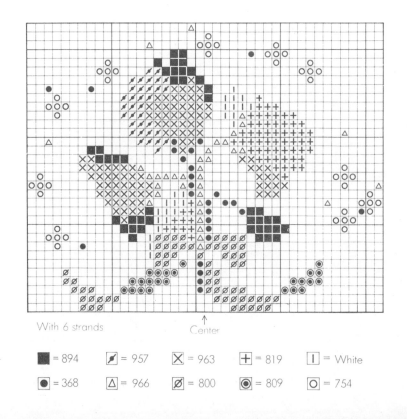

With 6 strands

Center

■ = 894	⚡ = 957	✕ = 963	✚ = 819	Ι = White
● = 368	△ = 966	∅ = 800	◉ = 809	○ = 754

POUCH *shown on page 38*

You'll Need:
- Fabric . . . Java cloth (10 cm of fabric = 35 square meshes) 29 cm by 22 cm Sky Blue.
- Threads . . . D.M.C 6-strand embroidery floss: ½ skein of White; small amount each of Peony Rose (957), Soft Pink (776), Saffron (727), Peacock Green (993), Brilliant Green (703) and Umber (433).
- Fittings . . . 1.2 cm wide bias tape Pink 30 cm long.

Finished Size: 12.5 cm by 9.5 cm

Size of Stitch: 1 square of design = 1 square mesh of fabric

Making Instructions:
Work embroidery matching center of front to that of design. Having stitched whole the design, sew referring to chart.

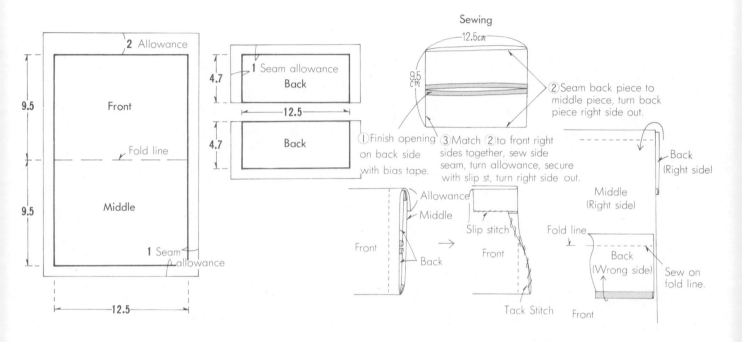

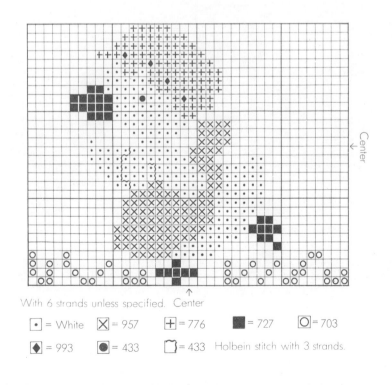

With 6 strands unless specified. Center

$\cdot$ = White	X = 957	+ = 776	■ = 727	O = 703
◆ = 993	● = 433	▢ = 433	Holbein stitch with 3 strands.	

Left

You'll Need:

· Fabrics . . . Java cloth (10 cm of fabric = 25 square meshes) 81 cm by 36 cm Beige. Cotton for lining 63 cm by 36 cm.

· Threads . . . D.M.C 6-strand embroidery floss:
1½ skeins of Soft Pink (776); 1 skein each of Emerald Green (913), Scarab Green (3348), Forget-me-not Blue (809), White; ½ skein each of Geranium Red (948), Tangerine Yellow (743), Peony Rose (956), Parma Violet (209), Sevres Blue (799), Geranium Pink (894), Umber Gold (976); small amount each of Peony Rose (957), Tangerine Yellow (742), Umber Gold (977) and Umber (435).

Finished Size: Refer to chart.

Size of Stitch: 1 square of design = 1 square mesh of fabric

Making Instructions:

Work embroidery on front where indicated. Having stitched embroidery, make referring to chart.

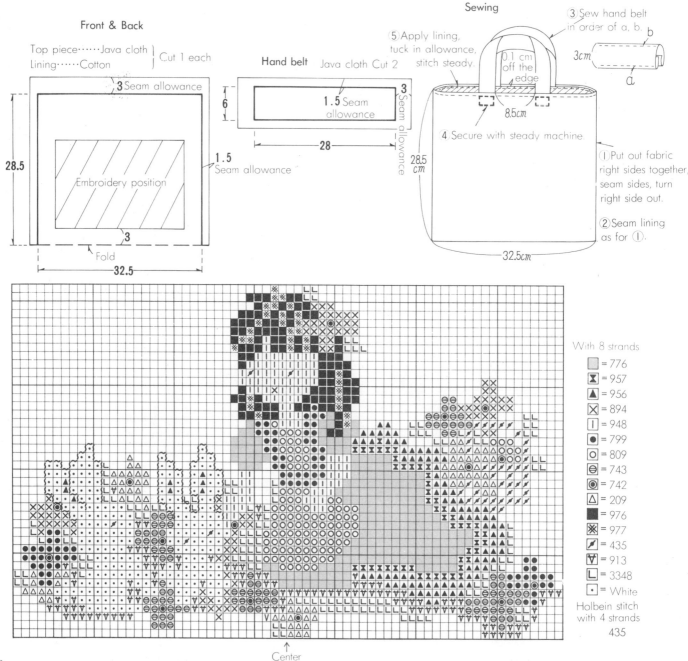

With 8 strands

▢	= 776
☒	= 957
▲	= 956
✕	= 894
❙	= 948
●	= 799
◯	= 809
⊖	= 743
◉	= 742
△	= 209
■	= 976
※	= 977
✦	= 435
⑂	= 913
L	= 3348
·	= White

Holbein stitch with 4 strands
435

Right

You'll Need:

· Fabrics . . . Java cloth (10 cm of fabric = 25 square meshes) 90 cm by 34 cm Cream. Cotton for lining 72 cm by 29 cm.
· Threads . . . D.M.C 6-strand embroidery floss:
2 skeins of Umber (435); 1½ skeins each of Peony Rose (956), White; 1 skein each of Soft Pink (818), Emerald Green (913); ½ skein each of Sevres Blue (799), Forget-me-not Blue (809), Scarab Green (3347), Emerald Green (955); small amount each of Geranium Red (948), Mahogany (301), Parma Violet (209) and Canary Yellow (972).

Finished Size: Refer to chart.
Size of Stitch: 1 square of design = 1 square mesh of fabric
Making Instructions:
Embroider design on front where indicated. Having stitched whole the design, make as for left bag.

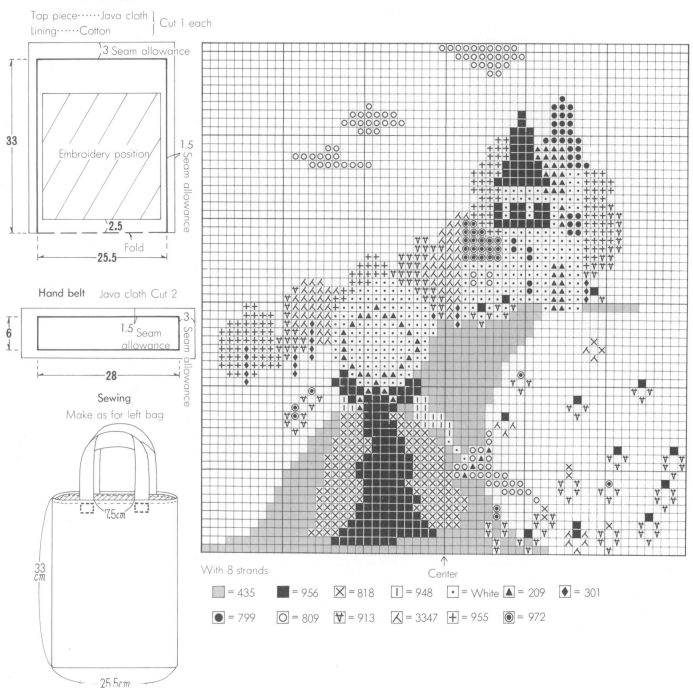

Front & Back

Top piece······Java cloth ⎫ Cut 1 each
Lining······Cotton ⎭

3 Seam allowance

33

Embroidery position

1.5 Seam allowance

2.5

Fold

25.5

Hand belt   Java cloth Cut 2

6

1.5 Seam allowance

3 Seam allowance

28

Sewing
Make as for left bag

7.5cm

33 cm

25.5cm

With 8 strands

= 435	= 956	☒ = 818

⌷ = 948   · = White   ▲ = 209   ◆ = 301

⊙ = 799   ◯ = 809   ∀ = 913   ⅄ = 3347   + = 955   ◉ = 972

Center

You'll Need:
- Fabrics . . . Indian cloth (10 cm of fabric = 52 square meshes) 90 cm by 65 cm Blue. Cotton for lining 51 cm by 19 cm.
- Threads . . . D.M.C 6-strand embroidery floss:
  2 skeins of Laurel Green (988); 1½ skeins of Scarab Green (3347); 1 skein of Beige Brown (840); ½ skein each of White, Scarab Green (3348); small amount each of Beige Brown (842), Coffee Brown (898), Soft Pink (899, 818), Peony Rose (957), Sky Blue (518, 519), Faded Pink (225), Umber (738), Saffron (727) and Ash Grey (414).
- Fittings . . . Interfacing 16 cm by 14 cm.

Finished Size: Refer to chart.
Size of Stitch: 1 square of design = 1 square mesh of fabric
Making Instructions:
Work embroidery matching center of design to that of pocket piece. Having stitched whole the design, sew referring to chart.

A

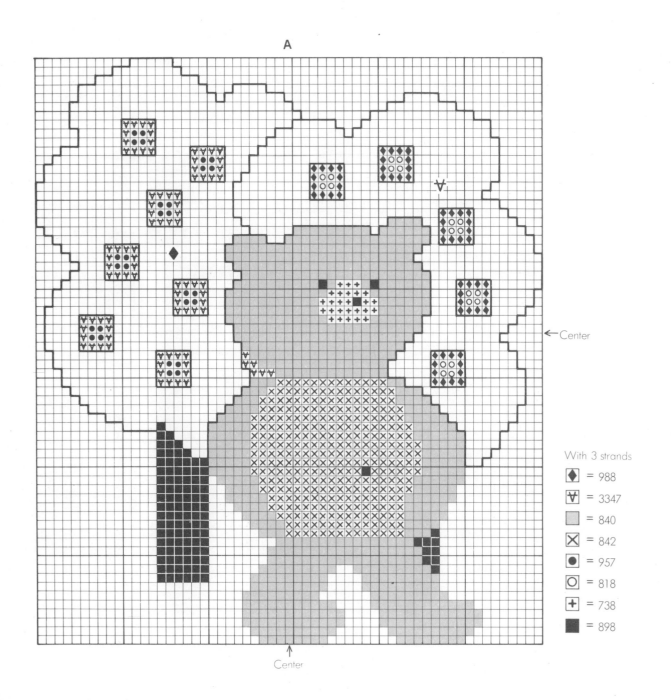

← Center

↑
Center

With 3 strands

◆	= 988
ⱽ	= 3347
(grey)	= 840
✕	= 842
●	= 957
○	= 818
+	= 738
■	= 898

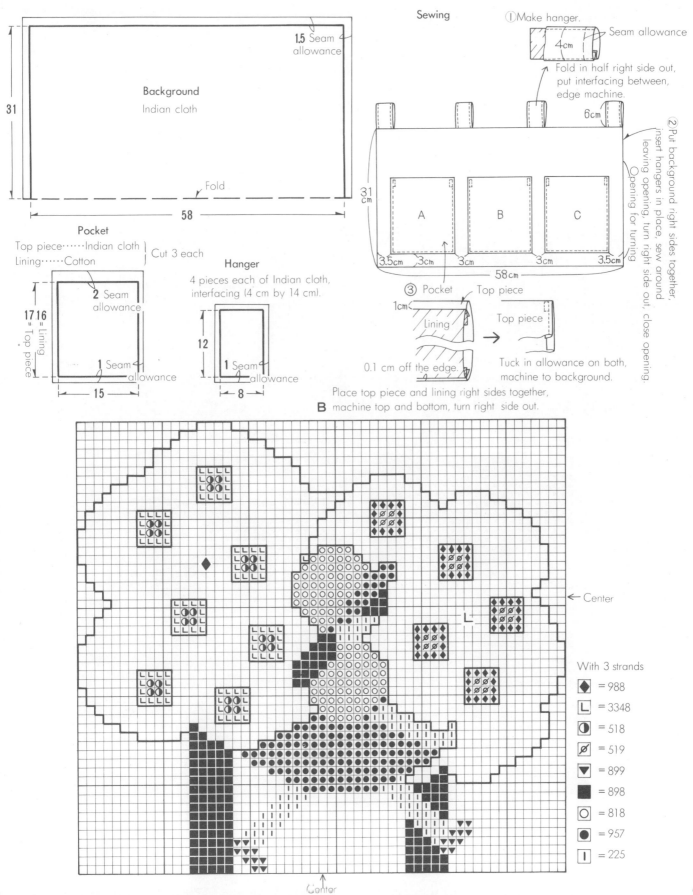

Background
Indian cloth

31

58

1.5 Seam allowance

Fold

Pocket

Top piece······Indian cloth
Lining······Cotton

Cut 3 each

17 = Lining
16 = Top piece

2 Seam allowance

1 Seam allowance

15

Hanger

4 pieces each of Indian cloth, interfacing (4 cm by 14 cm).

12

1 Seam allowance

8

Sewing

①Make hanger.

4cm

Seam allowance

Fold in half right side out, put interfacing between, edge machine.

6cm

②Put background right sides together, insert hangers in place, sew around leaving opening, turn right side out, close opening.

Opening for turning.

31 cm

A   B   C

3.5cm 3cm 3cm   3cm 3.5cm

58cm

③ Pocket   Top piece

1cm

Lining

0.1 cm off the edge.

Top piece

Tuck in allowance on both, machine to background.

Place top piece and lining right sides together,
B machine top and bottom, turn right side out.

Center

L

Center

With 3 strands

◆ = 988

L = 3348

◑ = 518

⊘ = 519

▼ = 899

■ = 898

○ = 818

● = 957

I = 225

C

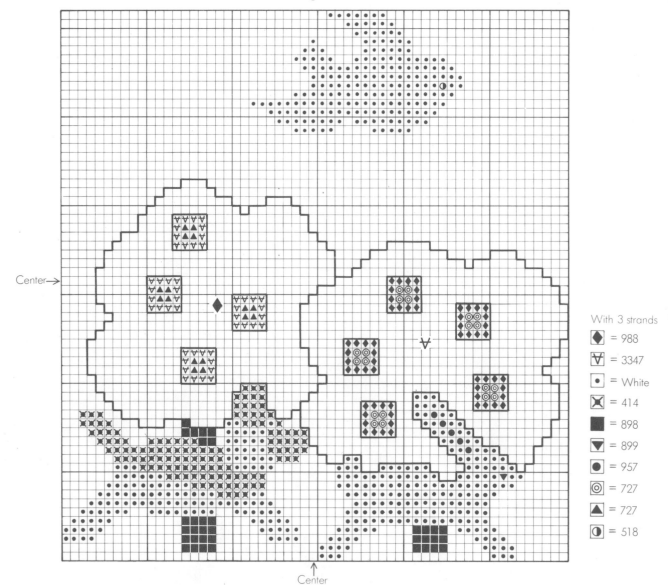

Center→

Center

With 3 strands

◆ = 988
∀ = 3347
• = White
✕ = 414
■ = 898
▼ = 899
● = 957
◎ = 727
▲ = 727
◗ = 518

BASICS

Cross Stitch

Make design working each stitch in the form of X orderly. It is important to make top stitch always lie in the same direction.

Select an even weave fabric (clearly woven square meshes) especially made for the purpose of cross stitch.

Use cross stitch needle the tip of which is blunt, so that it easily comes through meshes without splitting or picking up unnecessary threads.

Forming Stitches on Returning:

Bring out at lower left, insert in upper right.

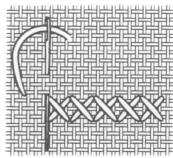

Having stitched to right edge of design, bring out at lower right, insert in upper left to form X on the line.

Having finished 1st row, go on to next row.

Forming Each Stitch Crosswise:

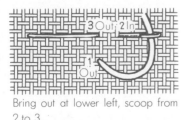

Bring out at lower left, scoop from 2 to 3.

Insert in lower right, bring out at 5 to form X.

Proceed sidelong making the X side by side.

Forming Each Stitch Lengthwise:

Bring out at upper right, scoop from 2 to 3.

Insert in lower right to form X, bring out at 5.

Scoop from 6 to 7 vertically.

Proceed upwards making the X side by side.
In case of proceeding downwards, care to make the stitch crossed over always lie in the same direction.

Proceeding Slantwise from Lower Left:

Bring out at 1, scoop crosswise 2 to 3.

Scoop from 4 to 5 vertically.

Proceed upwards right side, making X side by side.

Proceeding Slantwise from Upper Right:

Bring out at 1, scoop
2 to 3 vertically.

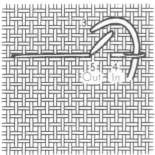

Scoop 4 to 5 horizontally.

Proceed toward lower
right, forming X one by
one.

Holbein Stitch

This stitch may be called line stitch, for it makes the outline of besign effective. The stitch is often worked in combination with cross stitch to form outlines or borders. The line is completed on returning. The finish of back side is same as front.

Straight Line:

Scoop fabric threads same
amount each.

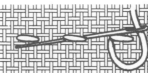

Having stitched to the edge of design, return filling the spaces between.
In order to get a neat result, try to work either way; bringing out at below
(or above) the former stitch, inserting at above (or below) the former stitch.

Slant Line:

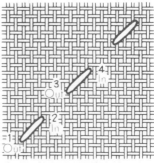

Stitch slantwise, making spaces
even.

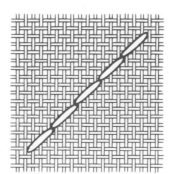

Having stitched to the end of design,
return in same manner as for straight line.

Step Line:

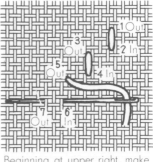

Beginning at upper right, make
vertical stitches.

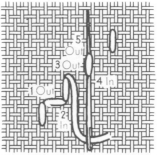

Bring out at 1, scoop 2 to 3.

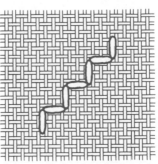

Form step line making horizontal
stitches on returning.

One-Side Hemstitching

Bring needle out at right near the edge of open-work, pick up three threads scooping right to left. Scoop fabric right near the picked up thread vertically, draw thread on the needle. Repeat.

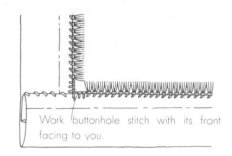

Work buttonhole stitch with its front facing to you.

Stitching Manner:

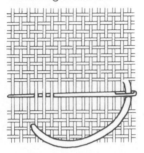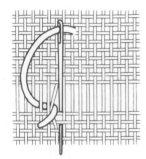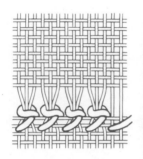

Mitering

①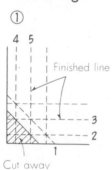

4 5

Finished line

3

2

1

Cut away

②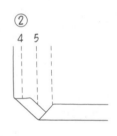

4 5

③

Slip stitch

Fold where indicated in numerical order.

Piping

①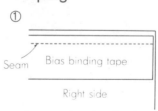

Seam

Bias binding tape

Right side

Seam applying bias binding.

② (Machined)

Bias binding tape

Steady machine.

Right side

Turn bias binding to wrong side, machine along the seam to finish.

(Back view)

Wrong side

② (Hand-sewn)

Bias binding tape

Wrong side

Turn bias binding to wrong side, secure with slip stitch.